THE RENAL PATIENT'S GUIDE TO GOOD EATING

A COOKBOOK FOR PATIENTS BY A PATIENT

ABOUT THE AUTHOR

Judith A. Curtis was raised in Honolulu, Hawaii, and as a teacher has been involved primarily in Early Childhood Education. Her interest in cooking and recipe collecting evolved over her 37 years as a Navy wife. She has traveled extensively all over the world and lived in Europe and the Orient. On several tours, she has helped edit and compile Navy wives' cookbooks for charity. A renal patient on dialysis since 1985, she received a kidney transplant in November, 1987. Mrs. Curtis lives in Hawaii with her husband, Navy Captain (Ret.) Robert E. Curtis.

Second Edition

THE RENAL PATIENT'S GUIDE TO GOOD EATING

A Cookbook for Patients by a Patient

By

JUDITH A. CURTIS

With a Foreword by

Judith A. Frank, R.D., C.S.R.

Illustrations by

Thomas Batis

CHARLES C THOMAS • PUBLISHER, LTD.
Springfield • Illinois • U.S.A.

Published and Distributed Throughout the World by

CHARLES C THOMAS • PUBLISHER, LTD.
2600 South First Street
Springfield, Illinois 62704

©2003 by CHARLES C THOMAS • PUBLISHER, LTD.

ISBN 0-398-07399-6 (spiral) paper

Library of Congress Catalog Card Number: 2003040176

Library of Congress Cataloging-in-Publication Data

Curtis, Judith A.
    The renal patient's guide to good eating : a cookbook for patients by
a patient / by Judith A. Curtis ; with a foreword by Judith A. Frank ;
illustrations by Thomas Batis.
      p. cm
    Includes bibliographical references and index.
    ISBN 0-398-07399-6 (spiral)
    1. Chronic renal failure--Diet therapy--Receipes. 2. Chronic renal
failure--Nutritional aspects. I. Title.

RC918.R4C88 2003
641.5'631--dc21
                                                                    2003040176

I dedicate this book to Bob, Mike and Cathy,
with love and appreciation for sharing the burden of
renal failure with me and for tolerating
my endless cooking experiments.

FOREWORD

"Could you give me some more ideas for meals?" This is the question often asked of the dietitian soon after the basic information on renal nutrition has been presented. Perhaps it stems from a desire to make up for all the restrictions and avoidances. Often the diet comes at the same time dialysis treatment is initiated. This is the period when discouragement can easily set in, leading to an inadequate diet or even abandonment of the restrictions altogether.

As a patient, Mrs. Curtis relates her own experience in dealing with the renal diet. Through a positive approach, she demonstrates that sometimes when you "make the best of it", the results are better than if the problem had not occurred. Fellow patients will recognize many of the author's feelings and obstacles as their own.

This cookbook is suitable for anyone. It does not separated the "dieters" from others. There will be no whispered requests for the salt shaker because the taste is there, in the form of herbs, spices, wine and other "allowed" flavorings. Especially valuable are the sections, where salt is typically relied upon heavily, namely, meat, fish, poultry, sandwiches and vegetables. There are recipes ranging from appetizers to desserts, quick and simple to the more elaborate. The author provides guidelines for adjusting to a healthy heart diet, as well as to renal diets, which require more or less stringency.

THE RENAL PATIENTS GUIDE TO GOOD EATING: A Cookbook for Patients by a Patient, is certain to enlighten and inspire anyone with kidney disease, from the newly diagnosed to the more experienced. Mrs. Curtis is to be commended for her honesty and creativity. I look forward to answering the patient's earlier mentioned request for ideas with, "I have just the book for you!"

JUDITH A. FRANK, R.D.

PREFACE

The second edition of THE RENAL PATIENT'S GUIDE TO GOOD EATING includes many new dishes as well as nutritional information for all recipes. This should make it easier for renal patients and their dietitians to determine how these dishes can best fit into their diet plans. The analyses can be used as a guide to appropriate serving sizes for each patient's daily allowances of sodium, potassium and phosphorus. The number of servings and amount per serving are given for comparison purposes only and are not meant to suggest that all patients would necessarily eat the amounts listed. Great care has been taken to include complete nutrition information whenever possible. However, due to the lack of nutrient values for certain foods, actual total may be higher than listed.

Note that protein sources (i.e., meat, poultry and seafood) contain significant amounts of potassium and/or phosphorus. It is important for renal patients to follow the protein recommendations given by their dietitian, as the values for these nutrients have been calculated into their meal plan.

It should also be noted that nutritional analyses for most of the sandwich recipes do not include nutrient values for the bread. The types of breat available vary widely in size and nutrient content. Once again, it is best to check with your dietitian.

Carbohydrate information in the analyses should provide an additional help to diabetic renal patients in the number and variety of recipes they can enjoy. For those not already familiar with "carb counting," a Certified Diabetes Educator or dietitian can give guidelines on this method of calculating foods for inclusion in the diabetic diet.

This revised edition of THE RENAL PATIENT'S GUIDE TO GOOD EATING would not have been possible without the guidance and help of the following individuals: My sincere thanks to:

- Judy Frank, RD, CSR, Nutrition Coordinator, Renal Institute of the Pacific, St. Francis Medical Center, for her thorough review of the recipes along with helpful suggestions and guidance.
- Anne Caprio Shovik, Ph.D., RD, Associate Professor, Human Nutrition, Food and Animal Science, University of Hawaii, for her assistance with resources.
- Angela Kusatsu, BS, dietetic intern and a recent graduate in Nutrition at the University of Hawaii, who so diligently carried out the tedious task of analyzing each recipe in this book.

To my fellow renal patients, may this collection of recipes add to the variety and number of dishes you can enjoy. Bon Appetit!

INTRODUCTION

One of the most difficult aspects of kidney failure for me was the extremely limited and complex diet I was advised to follow. The dietitian presented me with a seemingly endless list of restrictions on protein, sodium, potassium and phosphorus (which at the time I thought was found only in laundry detergent.) I left her office with so much technical information, so many "don'ts" and "no-no's" that I was both overwhelmed and depressed. As a diabetic, I was already on a sugar-restricted diet. With all of these new limitations, I really felt as if there was very little left I could eat, including many of my favorite foods. I also felt isolated from other family members and friends by the need for a "special diet" and initially prepared separate meals for myself.

During my three years on dialysis, I gradually evolved an eating plan that solved many of these problems without resorting to an isolation diet or throwing my laboratory blood chemistries out of whack. An avid cook and recipe collector, I decided that renal failure was not going to prevent me from enjoying two of my favorite pastimes, cooking and eating! I found, however, that there was not much available in the form of a comprehensive cookbook or guide for the kidney patient. The few available were very limited in the number and variety of recipes offered. Ordinary "diet" and "health" books, including my diabetic recipes, were also of limited value, containing many of the very foods I had to avoid as a kidney patient. (It seemed as if tomato sauce, dairy products, whole grains and potatoes were main ingredients in a majority of them.)

Still determined that a restricted diet shouldn't have to restrict good taste, I armed myself with the dietitian's nutrition lists, along with files of my favorite recipes, and set out to modify them. In many instances, I simply had to eliminate a few ingredients and substitute "legal" foods. In other cases, I started from scratch to come up with recipes that could be included in my diet. These efforts resulted in a surprising number and variety of dishes which, according to my family and friends, were tasteful and not at all diet-like.

Along with the modification and creation of recipes, I found many other ways to deal with my dietary restrictions. Mealtimes are more than just a time to eat; they are a social, sharing time as well. Kidney patients are faced with trying to fit their nutritional needs into their own individual lifestyles. In my case, being the wife of a Navy Officer meant lots of entertaining and eating out. It was one thing to follow my diet at home where I had control over what ingredients were used in cooking and entirely another when I went out. In time I learned to cope with these situations and many others, and I have included some of the things I learned as a part of this guide.

In discussing diet and the lack of available resources with other renal patients, it became apparent that they might benefit from my collection of recipes and hints on how I've come to cope with dietary restrictions. As a result, this cookbook was written. Hopefully, it will become a handy resource guide for your kitchen. There are a great number and variety of recipes, many of them collected from countries I've lived and traveled in around the world as a Navy wife. My goal in compiling this book has been to help other kidney patients make their mealtimes as pleasant as possible by providing recipes that they, their families and friends can enjoy together.

I should emphasize here that, as a renal patient, your own diet is dependent upon your body's ability to regulate blood constituents. The dietitian at your dialysis unit has either given you a tailor-made diet or at least guidelines as to what you can eat. Therefore, although the recipes included here are generally suitable for most renal patients, it is essential that you consult your dietitian as to how they can fit into your individual diet plan. This cookbook is not intended as a replacement for professional guidance, but rather as a supplement to expand the pleasurable possibilities of your renal diet.

ACKNOWLEDGMENTS

I am especially grateful to Judy Frank, R.D., my dietitian at the Renal Institute of the Pacific, St. Francis Medical Center, Honolulu, for her invaluable assistance in reviewing and analyzing the recipes in this book. Without her support and encouragement, this book would never have materialized. My deepest appreciation also to my nephrologists, Dr. Eugene Wong, Dr. Jared Sugihara, and Dr. Thomas Tasaki, for their exceptional medical skill and commitment to patient care in an often exhausting and stressful field of medicine. To the nurses and staff of the Renal Institute of the Pacific, St. Francis Medical Center, Honolulu, my heartfelt thanks for not only your care and support, but for your friendship as well. Finally, to my surgeons, Dr. Fong-Liang Fan and Dr. Livingston Wong, my eternal gratitude for the gift of a new lease on life and hope in the future.

CONTENTS

THE RENAL PATIENT'S GUIDE
TO GOOD EATING

Chapter 1

GUIDELINES TO LIVING
WITH A RENAL DIET

TAKE CONTROL OF YOUR OWN DIET

Perhaps the most important thing I've learned from my experience with kidney failure and dialysis, and more recently as a transplant recipient, is that I do have a great deal of control over my own well-being. My initial feelings of dependence on the medical staff of my dialysis center gradually gave way to a determination to do my best to return to as normal a lifestyle as possible. Even though I could not control what had happened to me, I could control how I dealt with it. It became a challenge, and often a fun one at that, to find ways of working with my restrictions.

As a first step towards taking control of your renal diet, become familiar with all those nutrition lists the dietitian gave you. If you're like me, they were initially so long and forbidding that I stuck them away in a drawer and avoided looking at them altogether. I tried to remember a few of the major "no-no's," and then proceeded to eat pretty much the same things I had eaten all along. Then the monthly phone calls from the renal dietitian began after each lab test: "Your phosphorus level's too high," or "You've got to watch that potassium; it's way up this month." These pronouncements were usually followed by dire predictions of what would happen to my already stressed body if I didn't watch my diet. ("Too much potassium can cause heart irregularities!") Finally, I decided it was time to take the nutrition lists seriously. It became a challenge to see how much I could learn about my renal diet, and I soon became an expert on what I could and couldn't eat.

You can start by using your nutrition list as a reference and guide. I found it helpful to take one group of foods (such as vegetables) at a time so you're not overwhelmed. If your dialysis center's list is very long and complex, make your own simplified version by grouping foods into low, moderate, and high categories of sodium, potassium, and phosphorus. Your dietitian will be happy to help you with this also. Soon, you will find that you have memorized a good portion of the list and you won't have to look at it so often.

When shopping for food, make a grocery list before you leave home. Use your diet list as a guide to what you should buy. This will also help to prevent impulse purchases (better for your pocketbook as well as your diet!). In the beginning I took my simplified "legal foods" sheet with me to the market. This prevented confusion in the fruit and vegetable section particularly. (Was it plums or nectarines I was supposed to avoid?)

Learn to use your nutrition list creatively to get out of the same old rut, using the same old foods you always have. Try new fruits and vegetables you may not have eaten before. I discovered won bok (Chinese cabbage), and it's now one of my favorite vegetables. Let's face it, the number and variety of allowable foods on a renal diet is limited enough without at least trying all of the ones you can eat. You can also create new recipes or modify old ones like I did to add variety to your diet.

COPING WITH THE RESTRICTIONS

Sodium

The word "salt" or "sodium" is usually the first element your dietitian says you must restrict. Dietary sodium affects fluid balance within the body. Healthy kidneys are able to excrete excess sodium and fluid from the body, but in kidney disease, a high sodium intake will cause retention of fluid. This fluid "overload" can result in weight gain, swelling, high blood pressure, and even shortness of breath due to accumulation of fluid around the lungs. This is also why we may be advised to restrict our fluid intake along with everything else on the list. The fact that salty foods cause thirst is just another reason to limit them in your diet. It has recently been well publicized that most American diets contain many times the amount of salt necessary to meet nutritional needs. Sodium occurs naturally in most foods. Over the years, however, people have acquired a taste for salty food, and this has resulted in a food industry that relies on heavy doses of added salt for flavor and public appeal. This becomes painfully obvious only when you have to start watching your salt intake like renal patients do.

Your dietitian will have given you a complete list of foods and their sodium content, along with the maximum amount of sodium you should consume each day. Again, it is to your benefit to become familiar with this list. You cannot always determine sodium content by taste. I was amazed to learn that a cup of cornflakes contains more sodium than a strip of bacon! Several examples of high sodium foods are pizza, frozen dinners, canned soups, pickled vegetables, luncheon meats and frankfurters, smoked or cured products, and cheeses.

The most obvious way to decrease sodium in cooking is simply not to use it. The cooking directions for pasta, vegetables, and cereals call for adding salt to the cooking water. You can easily omit the salt without losing much flavor. In most recipes, you can leave the salt out altogether to begin with and then add a little to taste later if necessary. With this in mind, I have intentionally eliminated the use of salt in all of my recipes for this cookbook. Your individual sodium restriction and dietitian's advice will determine whether you can add salt and how much.

Rinsing foods also gets rid of excess sodium. The salt content of canned foods such as tuna and vegetables can be significantly reduced by putting them in a strainer and rinsing for a minute or so under running water.

In dealing with your sodium restriction, you will learn right away that cooking from "scratch" is often the only way to reduce salt in your diet. We have become so used to using convenience foods, either packaged or frozen, and unfortunately most of them are extremely high in sodium. Cooking without using prepared or processed foods is not as difficult or as time-consuming as it may sound. Many of the recipes in this book are quick and easy to prepare, and you will find your own shortcuts. When you do have some extra time, cook and freeze some meals or main dishes for future use. I also find it helpful to prepare part of the evening meal ahead of time (such as chopping vegetables, slicing or chopping meat, making sauces, etc.). Then, all you have to do at the last minute is assemble and cook the final dish. It's even easier if you own a microwave oven. I will often prepare the entire entree in the morning, refrigerate it, and then pop it in the microwave just before serving.

Another way to reduce sodium in your diet is to use the wide variety of no- or low-salt products now on the market. Fortunately for kidney patients, the recent link between sodium consumption and high blood pressure in the general population has led to a new demand for less salt in foods. Look for the following in reduced or no sodium versions: mayonnaise, baking powder, soy sauce, butter and margarine, salad dressings, and snack items (crackers, cookies, pretzels, chips, etc.). Many commercial, low-sodium seasonings are also available: lemon-pepper mixtures, salt-free steak sauce, all-purpose seasonings and herb seasonings for meats, poultry, fish, etc. Avoid using salt substitutes which contain potassium chloride, a definite "no-no" for kidney patients. While I have not specifically referred to use of low sodium products (i.e., mayonnaise, butter, etc.) in all of my recipes, you can easily substitute them if your particular diet demands it.

With the reduced use of salt in your cooking and at the table, many dishes will taste bland at first. As sodium intake decreases, however, your taste buds will adjust and craving for salt will diminish. You will begin to discover what food really tastes like without salt masking the flavor. I find now that I actually prefer dishes that aren't heavily salted because the subtle, natural flavors and seasonings come through.

Try experimenting with different flavor enhancers that will help you eliminate salt without sacrificing taste. Some of my favorite seasonings include fresh and dried herbs, spices, wine, flavored vinegars, lemon juice, fresh-ground pepper, and garlic. In dishes calling for onion and garlic salt, use onion and garlic powder instead. As the recipes in this cookbook demonstrate, these seasonings can be used in many ways to add interest and variety to your meals. You can try your own seasoning blends, keeping in mind that the "light touch" is best. I found out when I was experimenting with spices and herbs that they can overpower a dish if you're not careful. The purpose is to enhance foods' natural flavors, not mask them.

The Two "P's"–Potassium and Phosphorus

Renal diets go much further than simple sodium restriction. It is also essential that we watch our potassium and phosphorus levels. My dietitian told me that the diseased kidney cannot regulate these elements in the blood and that they are also not adequately removed by dialysis. Thus, dietary restriction is essential.

When I was handed these lists, I *really* became depressed! I had never oversalted my food or used much in cooking. But here in front of me were what seemed like pages of my favorite foods with big red "X's" in front of them. No-no's in the potassium category included tomatoes, potatoes, nuts, avocados, broccoli, bananas, and oranges. The list for phosphorus was equally devastating: milk and other dairy products, dried beans, nuts, and whole grains.

What's Left That I Can Eat?

As I've detailed elsewhere, these initial feelings of complete deprivation and impending starvation were eventually overcome by really studying my nutrition lists and finding out exactly what I could and couldn't eat. There are fruits and vegetables you can have, and while the quantity of dairy products and meats may not be what you're accustomed to, they can still be a part of your diet. Even though the person who handed you all those horrible "no-no" lists may seem like an enemy at first, your dietitian is in reality the one who can assist you in coping with your limitations. She has your best health and well-being at heart and is more than anxious to help you adjust to your diet. Look at it from her point of view, too. Imagine having to face the wrath and indignation of patient after patient, day after day, as she tells them about their new diets! Ask questions and listen to her suggestions; you will be surprised at the help and resources that are available.

As I mentioned earlier, your dietitian can also be your best guide as to how this cookbook can fit into your diet plan. Most of the recipes come from the "low" and "moderate" categories of sodium, potassium, and phosphorus. They can for the most part be used on even the most restricted diets. If your particular eating plan is not so severely limited, you can add a little salt here, a bit of cheese there to suit your own taste and diet.

Quantity of food consumed can be just as important as quality. This will vary widely from one individual to another, depending on each person's daily protein allowance. A kitchen scale is invaluable in helping you to weigh out your allowable portion of meat.

Because of the restrictions on protein intake, carbohydrates and fats make up a good percentage of the renal patient's diet. The calories they provide are helpful in maintaining weight and energy levels. Most kidney patients can enjoy the sugars and fats so often restricted in other foods containing sugar; corn syrup, honey, and butter are allowed. Thus, sweet desserts can be a part of most renal diets. With your physician's okay, alcoholic beverages within your fluid allowance can occasionally be enjoyed also.

A Word to Diabetics

If you are a diabetic, as I am, you face even greater restrictions, including all those sugars and rich desserts described earlier. Many of the recipes in this cookbook are suitable for inclusion in a diabetic diet, although no attempt has been made to eliminate all sugar. I have been able to tolerate small amounts of sugar in my diet, but this may not be the case for all diabetics. If your particular diet dictates it, you can substitute artificial sweetener for sugar in many of the recipes.

A Word About Fats and Cholesterol

During the time I was on dialysis, my husband underwent coronary by-pass surgery. Then, he was the one who came home with yet another list of restrictions pertaining to fats and cholesterol. Of course, this did not coincide with *my* lists which limited just about everything else but allowed fat!

If you are faced with a similar problem or need to be concerned about your own heart's health, here are some suggestions based on general guidelines from the American Heart Association:

1. Use fish, chicken, turkey, and veal more often than beef, lamb, and pork. Substitute chicken or turkey breasts in recipes that call for

veal steaks or cutlets. Restrict your use of luncheon and variety meats (hot dogs, bologna, salami, etc.), most of which are not allowed on renal diets either.

2. When choosing ground beef, look for low fat content. Ground beef should contain no more than 10 percent fat. You can also buy your own lean beef and have the butcher grind it for you or grind it yourself at home. Ground turkey and chicken are now readily available and these lower fat poultry items can be substituted for ground beef in most recipes.

3. Use polyunsaturated or monounsaturated vegetable oils in salad dressings and for cooking. The polyunsaturates include safflower, soybean, sunflower, and corn oil. Olive oil and peanut oil are primarily monounsaturated. Watch out for palm kernel oil and coconut oil in processed foods. Both are very high in saturated fats.

4. Substitute margarine for butter at the table and in cooking. Preferred margarines are those which list liquid oil as the first ingredient.

5. Select fat-free or low-fat dairy products among those that are allowed on your renal diet. Avoid whole eggs whenever possible. Two egg whites can be substituted for one whole egg in most recipes. Egg whites alone can also be used in recipes that call for an egg dip before breading.

6. Roasting, baking, broiling, braising, and sautéing are recommended cooking methods. Trim all visible fat from meats before cooking. Microwaving is also recommended.

7. Emphasize complex carbohydrates, such as bread, rice, and pasta in your meal planning.

THE SOCIAL SIDE OF LIVING WITH YOUR DIET

Dining At Home

Your family's adjustment to your diet regimen is almost as important as yours. Initially, I felt that there was no way I could impose my restrictions on the rest of the family, so I prepared two meals each evening, one for them and one for me. Not only did this take an inordinate amount of time, it also left me feeling isolated and sorry for myself.

It was at this point that I decided to experiment with new recipes and modification on old ones. If you do this gradually, your family won't even notice that they are eating more or less of certain vegetables or fruits, or that tomato sauce isn't a main ingredient at mealtimes any more. My family even stopped missing potatoes every night when they discovered how good pasta and rice can be fixed in different ways.

The lack of salt will probably be the most noticeable change in your meals. Tell your family to add it to their food at the table if they like. They will eventually get used to less and prefer it that way. I noticed that the salt shaker was used less and less as time went on.

For those times when the family begs for your old ham and cheese casserole, have something on hand in the freezer you can fix for yourself. I would package up leftover sliced meat, rice, and the like for just such occasions. As long as I wasn't having to do this every night, I didn't mind it once in awhile. And if the ham and cheese casserole was *your* favorite as well, go ahead and have a bite or two. It won't hurt as long as you don't make a meal of it.

You can also entertain at home and still stay on your diet. The trend in eating for almost everyone today is away from the old "meat and potatoes" routine. I have included a lot of recipes in this book that are great for company, and you will find that you can use some of your own with a few modifications. Once again, point out the salt shaker to your guests. Since my friends still asked for my recipes after I went on dialysis, I figured my experimenting was a success. Remember also that people aren't going to notice that you're not serving broccoli or cream sauce or that you have left the celery out of the salad.

Dining In Restaurants

While you have a great deal of control over what you eat and prepare at home, it's a completely different story when you eat out. Many a restaurant can lead to the downfall of your renal diet! It's unfortunately still common to get extra-large portions and over-salted food in many establishments. If you have some say in the matter, select a restaurant that serves broiled, grilled or roasted meats and fresh vegetables and salads.

Even if you don't have a choice or don't know what a restaurant is like before you go, you can still ask questions and make requests once you're there. I have found that most places are very cooperative about telling how their food is prepared and modifying your selection if it's at all possible. I always ask that foods such as salad dressing, sauces, gravies, catsup, and mustard be served "on the side" so I can control the amount used. I also request unsalted food, and many restaurants are able to comply.

You can also stick to your diet when eating out by selecting plain meats and vegetables and avoiding casseroles and combination dishes. Salad bars can offer good choices if you remember your legal vegetables and fruits and make careful selections. Avoid the prepared salads with dressing and mayonnaise already added; they tend to have a lot of added sodium. On occasion I will bring my own low-salt salad dressing and unsalted crackers from home. If not, I use plain oil and vinegar or a very small amount of any other dressing.

There are also a number of ways to get around the too-ample helpings of food that some restaurants serve. Sometimes, with family or friends, we order several appetizers, then split the entree. Or, we will order two entrees for three people. This not only cuts down on the amount of food, but also gives you a chance to taste several dishes. I'm also not shy about asking for a "doggy bag" when I'm unable to eat all the food I have ordered. This is an accepted practice today, and most restaurants are happy to oblige.

There will be occasions when you don't have such choices and you know beforehand that the food you will be eating is going to throw you off your diet. The office is going out for pizza or your friends insist you join them for Chinese food. Instead of declining a fun invitation or sitting there not eating at all, just plan to be very strict about your diet for the rest of the day. Remember that it's day-to-day, long-term eating plan that counts.

Dining With Friends

Eating at friends' homes can be even more hazardous to your renal diet than restaurants, because you don't have a variety of choices. Whether you tell your host/hostess of your restrictions will depend on the circumstances. If you are the only guest invited, you can probably feel comfortable mentioning your diet. If the invitation is to a dinner party for several guests, I usually don't say anything when accepting the invitation. I don't want the host/hostess to feel obligated to change the menu or prepare something special for me. I usually will say something privately after I arrive so she'll know why I'm not eating certain foods.

Hopefully, you won't have the experience I did at a friend's home where absolutely everything on the menu, from appetizer to dessert, was from my mental list of "no-no's"! All I could see were big red "X's" from my renal diet booklet over all the food. I ate a very little of everything and completed my meal at home. It was after that experience that I began to be especially strict with the rest of my meals on days I planned on going out to dinner.

At cocktail parties there are usually plenty of choices and you have more control over what you eat. Choose from your legal list of raw vegetables and fruits and fresh sliced meats. Remember also that with your physician's permission, you are allowed to indulge in limited amounts of beer, wine, and liquor.

Potluck dinners also offer lots of choices and you can pick and choose what you eat. To be on the safe side, I usually take something I know I can eat and then sample small portions of other dishes.

SHOPPING TIPS

In addition to the shopping guidelines mentioned elsewhere in this book (making grocery lists and avoiding premixed, packaged "convenience" foods), there are a few other hints I picked up when I began my renal diet. If there are only two words I would like for you to remember as an aid in shopping, they would be: READ LABELS. Figuring out what the terms on food labels really mean isn't always easy. But if you know some basics and a few key terms, you can successfully navigate your way through the food-label jungle.

Ingredient lists provide helpful information in that ingredients are listed in order of highest to lowest amount, by weight. So if salt is one of the first items listed on the label, you know you should avoid that product. Not all foods have ingredient lists, but most do.

Along with ingredient lists, labeling laws now require food manufacturers to include nutrition information on their labels. In most cases, the exact amount of sodium per serving is given in milligrams. The Food and Drug Administration (FDA) has developed the following guidelines to make sodium labeling less confusing:

Sodium free: less than five milligrams sodium per serving.

Very low sodium: 25 milligrams or less sodium per serving.

Low sodium: 140 milligrams or less sodium per serving.

Reduced sodium: Sodium content reduced by at least 75 percent. The food label must show the sodium content of both the normal product and the reduced-sodium product.

Unsalted, no salt added, without added salt: No salt has been added to a product normally processed with salt.

Many labels are now including potassium content of the product as well. You can get a rough idea of the phosphorus level by its inclusion in the "Percentage of U.S. Recommended Daily Allowance" portion of nutrition labels. Protein is listed there also in grams per serving.

Another discovery I made when I started shopping as a renal patient was health food stores. These places are wonderful sources of low sodium products. You have to be careful, however, in that a lot of their nutritious food is loaded with potassium and phosphorus (whole grains, nuts, dried fruits, and beans). Fortunately, most health food companies are good at providing comprehensive nutrition labeling, and this will help you in your shopping.

A WORD ABOUT ATTITUDE AND OUTLOOK

I'm not going to deny that even after all my recipe modifications, culinary experimentation, and other methods of coping with my diet, I still don't often envy those who can eat anything they like. There is no getting around the fact that a renal diet is definitely a very restricted one. There will no doubt be some of your favorite foods listed among those you must restrict or eliminate entirely. (For me, artichokes, cheese, melons, and nuts were hardest to give up.) We all have times when we think it may not be worth it. These are the times when the temptations to forget your renal diet are the strongest. It's so easy to feel sorry for yourself and then to indulge in a "consolation prize" in the form of a double cheeseburger, fries, and a chocolate shake!

Take heart, though; eventually your tastes will change. You will develop new food favorites from the "legal" lists and lose your craving for salt. The benefits of sticking to your diet will far outweigh the momentary pleasure of a large meal from a fast food restaurant. You have to find your own reasons for committing yourself to following your diet. For me, it was a combination of wanting to look and feel as good as possible. It was reward enough whenever someone would say, "I can't believe there's a thing wrong with you!"

Know that your life can still be productive, effective, and a blessing to others despite the fact that you have kidney disease. You can play a positive, creative role in your own case. You may not be able to control what has happened to you, but you can control your attitude and outlook. We all lose certain battles in life, but the war of the spirit and mind can be won through faith, hope, and perseverance.

This cookbook is an attempt to give you psychological as well as physical benefits from following an eating plan that is delicious despite the restrictions. With a wide variety of recipes to choose from, perhaps you will be better motivated, as I was, to follow your diet. When confronted with kidney disease, we're told by the health care professionals to take control of our eating. It's up to us to meet this challenge in a positive manner. Hopefully, this cookbook can help make a difference between your merely surviving with renal failure and living life to its fullest. A quote from minister and author, Robert Schuller, has helped my to deal with my disease in general:

"Look not at what you have lost, but what you have left."

Concerning our renal diets, I would change this to:

*"Look not at what you **can't** eat, but what you **can!**"*

Chapter 2

APPETIZERS
AND BEVERAGES

Aloha Pineapple Dip

1 fresh pineapple
8 oz. cream cheese
1 sm. can crushed pineapple

Cut large opening in one side of pineapple. Scoop out insides, leaving pineapple shell hollow. Drain crushed pineapple and blend with cheese until smooth. Lay pineapple shell on it side and fill with cheese mixture. Serve with unsalted crackers.

12 servings. Serving size: 2 T. Per serving: 61 calories, 7 g total fat (4 g saturated),
2 g protein, 7 g carbohydrate, 57 mg sodium, 78 mg potassium, 23 mg phosphorus.

Boned Chicken Bits

4 chicken breasts
½ c. breadcrumbs
½ tsp. thyme
Pinch of basil
1 tsp. oregano
Pepper to taste
3 T. Parmesan cheese
Melted butter

Skin and bone chicken breasts; cut into small pieces. Dip into melted butter. Combine all other ingredients and roll chicken in this mixture. Bake at 400 degrees for 20 min.

18 servings. Serving size: 2 T. Per serving: 52 calories, 2 g total fat (1 g saturated), 7 g protein, 2 g carbohydrate, 64 mg sodium, 58 mg potassium, 58 mg phosphorus.

Chicken Pate

1½ c. finely chopped,
     cooked chicken
½ (8 oz.) pkg. cream cheese,
     softened
3 T. chopped onion
2 T. dry sherry
2 T. mayonnaise
2 tsp. lemon juice
¼ tsp. hot pepper sauce
⅛ tsp. nutmeg
Paprika

Combine ingredients (except paprika) in blender. Blend until smooth. Lightly grease a 2 cup mold; fill with blender mixture. Cover and chill overnight. Unmold onto serving plate, sprinkle with paprika. Serve with melba toast or unsalted crackers.

24 servings. Serving size: 2 T. Per serving: 35 calories, 3 g total fat (1 g saturated), 2 g protein, 0 g carbohydrate, 25 mg sodium, 22 mg potassium, 15 mg phosphorus.

Curried Beef Rolls with Chutney Dipping Sauce

1 lb. lean ground beef
1/4 tsp. ground black pepper
3 to 4 tsp. curry powder
1/2 tsp. cumin
1/2 tsp. cayenne pepper
2 T. fresh lemon juice
16 large leaves romaine lettuce
Chutney Dipping Sauce:
2 1/4 c. light sour cream
4 1/2 T. mango chutney,
   finely chopped
11 1/2 T. fresh lemon juice

Brown meat in large skillet over low heat. Season with pepper. Drain all but 1 T. fat. Add curry powder, cumin, and cayenne. Continue cooking and stirring 2 to 3 minutes. Remove from heat. Stir in the 2 T. lemon juice. Set aside.

Prepare **Chutney Dipping Sauce**: Stir sour cream, chutney and the 1 1/2 T. lemon juice in bowl. Add 1/3 c. of this mixture to meat; still well. Store remaining sauce in refrigerator.

Blanch lettuce leaves by plunging them in large post of boiling water for 5 seconds; then rinse with cold water to stop cooking. Cut each lettuce leaf in half lengthwise and remove thick center stem. You will need a piece, about 4 to 5 inches by 2 1/2 to 3 inches for each roll. Spoon 1 1/2 to 2 tsp. meat filling onto a short end of each lettuce leaf. Roll up, tucking in sides. Place, seam-side down, on serving plate. Serve with remaining dipping sauce.

16 servings. Serving size: 2 rolls. Per serving: 50 calories, 2 g total fat (2 g saturated), 2 g protein, 6 g carbohydrate, 17 mg sodium, 67 mg potassium, 35 mg phosphorus.

Dilly Shrimp Dip

4 1/2 oz. can shrimp, rinse and
  drained
Juice of 1/2 lemon
8 oz. pkg. cream cheese, softened
Fresh ground pepper
1/4 c. mayonnaise
2 T. finely chopped green onion
1/2 tsp. dried dillweed
1/2 tsp. hot pepper sauce
1/4 c. milk

Combine shrimp and lemon juice in small bowl and toss well. Drain; chop shrimp. Combine remaining ingredients until smooth. Add shrimp and stir to mix.

16 servings. Serving size: 2 T. Per serving: 88 calories, 8 g total fat (4 g saturated), 3 g protein, 1 g carbohydrate, 78 mg sodium, 50 mg potassium, 39 mg phosphorus.

Eggplant "Caviar"

1 large eggplant
2 T. olive oil
1 small onion, minced
1 clove garlic, minced
1/4 c. green pepper, minced
1 1/2 T. lemon juice

Slice eggplant in half and rub with 1 T. of the oil. Place halves cut side down on baking pan. Broil on middle rack of oven for 20 to 25 minutes or until soft. Cool slightly. Scoop out pulp and mash well with fork. Saute onion and garlic in remaining oil until brown. Stir into eggplant pulp with remaining ingredients. Chill for 2 or 3 hours. Sprinkle with chopped parsley and serve with bread rounds or toast.

16 servings. Serving size: 2 T. Per serving: 27 calories, 2 g total fat (0 g saturated), 0 g protein, 3 g carbohydrate, 1 mg sodium, 96 mg potassium, 10 mg phosphorus.

Frosted Zucchini Rounds

3 medium zucchini
1/2 c. mayonnaise
1/4 c. minced green onion
3 T. Parmesan cheese
1/2 tsp. oregano
1/8 tsp. garlic powder
Dash of pepper
1/4 c. unsalted cracker crumbs

Cut zucchini crosswise into 3/4-inch slices. Arrange slices in single layer in a vegetable steamer. Cover and steam over boiling water until barely tender, about 5 minutes. Drain, cook and blot dry. Mix mayonnaise, green onion, Parmesan, oregano, garlic, and pepper. Frost 1 side of each zucchini slice with the mayonnaise mixture, then dip top in cracker crumbs. Place on a cookie sheet, top side up. Broil about 4 inches from heat until lightly browned, about 3 to 6 minutes. Makes about 24.

12 servings. Serving size: 2 slices. Per serving: 88 calories, 8 g total fat (1 g saturated), 2 g protein, 3 g carbohydrate, 94 mg sodium, 162 mg potassium, 38 mg phosphorus.

Herbed Cream Cheese

2 lg. pkg cream cheese, softened
2 garlic cloves, crushed
1 tsp. dill
1 tsp. chervil
1/2 tsp. freshly ground pepper

In mixer bowl or food processor combine all ingredients until well mixed. Serve with raw vegetables or unsalted crackers.

16 servings. Serving size: 2 T. Per serving: 100 calories, 10 g total fat (6 g saturated), 2 g protein, 1 g carbohydrate, 85 mg sodium, 38 mg potassium, 30 mg phosphorus.

Marinated Shrimp

3 c. water
1 lb. medium shrimp
1 med. onion, minced
1 clove garlic, minced
¼ c. plus 2 T. low-sodium
  Italian dressing
3 T. dry white wine
3 T. lemon juice
¼ tsp. pepper
¼ tsp. hot sauce

Cook shrimp according to package directions. Drain and chill. Combine remaining ingredients in large bowl. Add shrimp, cover and refrigerate at least 8 hours or overnight, stirring occasionally. Drain and serve with toothpicks.

12 servings. Serving size: 3 pieces. Per serving: 56 calories, 1 g total fat (0 g saturated), 8 g protein, 3 g carbohydrate, 100 mg sodium, 95 mg potassium, 81 mg phosphorus.

Meatballs With Cucumber Dip

Meatballs:

1 lb. ground lamb
$1/2$ lb. ground beef
1 med. onion, minced
$1/4$ c. dry bread crumbs
1 T. chopped parsley
2 tsp. ground cumin

Preheat oven to 400 degrees. In a large bowl combine all ingredients. Shape into 1-inch balls and place in jelly-roll pan. Bake 12 to 15 minutes or until cooked through. Makes about 55 meatballs.

18 servings. Serving size: 3 meatballs. Per serving: 81 calories, 5 g total fat (2 g saturated), 6 g protein, 2 g carbohydrate, 34 mg sodium, 101 mg potassium, 54 mg phosphorus.

Dip:

1 (3 oz.) pkg. cream cheese, softened
$1/4$ c. plain yogurt
1 garlic clove, crushed
1 c. peeled, seeded and finely chopped cucumber

In small bowl beat cream cheese until soft. Stir in remaining ingredients. Cover and refrigerate.

18 servings. Serving size: $1 1/2$ T. Per serving: 20 calories, 2 g total fat (1 g saturated), 1 g protein, 1 g carbohydrate, 17 mg sodium, 23 mg potassium, 13 mg phosphorus.

Mexican Nibbles

1 egg white, room temp.
2½ tsp. chili powder
½ tsp. cumin
¼ tsp. garlic powder
3 c. Corn Chex® cereal

Beat egg white until foamy. Combine next 3 ingredients in bowl, stir well; fold into egg white. Add cereal, stir gently to coat. Spread mixture on lightly greased cookie sheet. Bake at 325 degrees for 15 minutes, stirring every 5 minutes. Cool on sheet. Store tightly covered. Makes 6 cups.

24 servings. Serving size: 1/4 cup. Per serving: 16 calories, 0 g total fat (0 g saturated), 0 g protein, 3 g carbohydrate, 39 mg sodium, 11 mg potassium, 3 mg phosphorus.

Oriental Meatballs

1 T. sherry
1 T. low-salt soy sauce
⅛ tsp. sesame hot oil
¼ c. water
½ clove garlic, minced
½ tsp. ginger
1 lb. lean ground beef

In a large bowl, combine first 6 ingredients. Add ground beef and mix lightly. Form into 1-inch balls. Arrange on a lightly greased baking dish. Bake at 450 degrees for 15 minutes. Serve with toothpicks. About 32 meatballs.

16 servings. Serving size: 2 meatballs. Per serving: 59 calories, 4 g total fat (1 g saturated), 6 g protein, 0 g carbohydrate, 46 mg sodium, 57 mg potassium, 32 mg phosphorus.

Parmesan Chips

1lb. lasagna noodles
1/4 c. vegetable oil
1/4 c. water
1/3 c. Parmesan cheese
2 tsp. basil, crushed
2 tsp. oregano, crushed
2 tsp. dried parsley, crushed
3/4 tsp. garlic powder

Cook noodles according to package directions; drain and separate on paper towels. Combine oil and water, brush both sides of noodles. Cut noodles crosswise into 2 inch pieces; arrange in single layer on lightly greased baking sheets. Set aside.

Combine Parmesan cheese and spices in small bowl. Sprinkle 1/8 tsp. of herb mix over each noodle. Bake at 400 degrees for 15 minutes or until crisp and golden. Cool and store in airtight container. Yields 12 dozen.

36 servings. Serving size: 4 chips. Per serving: 59 calories, 2 g total fat (0 g saturated), 2 g protein, 8 g carbohydrate, 21 mg sodium, 12 mg potassium, 30 mg phosphorus.

Quick Appetizer

Cream cheese (any size)
Green pepper or jalapeno jelly

Spoon jelly over block of slightly softened cream cheese. Serve with unsalted crackers.

9 servings. Serving size: 2 T. Per serving: 104 calories, 9 g total fat (6 g saturated), 2 g protein, 5 g carbohydrate, 77 mg sodium, 34 mg potassium, 27 mg phosphorus.

Roasted Garlic Spread

Preheat oven to 350 degrees F. Remove outer layer of skin from 6 heads of garlic. Cut ½ inch off from each head straight across top and arrange in shallow baking pan. Drizzle 2 tsp. olive oil over each head, letting it run between the cloves. Cover with foil and bake 30 minutes. Remove foil and bake 30 to 45 minutes more, until garlic is tender when pierced with a toothpick. Cool slightly. To serve, peel off cloves and squeeze the roasted garlic onto toasted rounds of bread or vegetables.

6 servings. Serving size: 1 bulb. Per serving: 124 calories, 9 g total fat (1 g saturated), 2 g protein, 10 g carbohydrate, 5 mg sodium, 120 mg potassium, 46 mg phosphorus.

Stuffed Lychees

Drain can of lychees and remove seeds. Stuff with small amount of cream cheese (a melon baller works well).

12 servings. Serving size: 1 piece. Per serving: 15 calories, 1 g total fat (1 g saturated), 0 g protein, 2 g carbohydrate, 7 mg sodium, 19 mg potassium, 5 mg phosphorus.

Stuffed Mushrooms

12 large white mushrooms,
   cleaned and dried with
   paper towels
2 T. chopped chives or
   green onion tops
2 T. reduced-fat mayonnaise
3 T. fat-free sour cream
2 T. grated Parmesan cheese
5 T. Italian seasoned bread crumbs
1 T. Balsamic vinegar
2-3 drops hot pepper sauce
   (optional)

Preheat the broiler. Spray a baking sheet with nonstick cooking spray. Trim the mushroom stems. Pull out the stems, chop and reserve. Lay the mushrooms rounded side down on the baking sheet. In a small bowl combine $1/3$ c. of the mushroom stems, chives, mayonnaise, sour cream, cheese, bread crumbs, vinegar and hot pepper sauce (if desired). Stir to mix well.

Stuff each mushroom with the cheese mixture. Broil 2 inches from broiler until the stuffing begins to brown, about 2 to 4 minutes. Serve warm.

12 servings. Serving size: 1 mushroom. Per serving: 37 calories, 1 g total fat (0 g saturated), 2 g protein, 5 g carbohydrate, 82 mg sodium, 151 mg potassium, 53 mg phosphorus.

Vegetable Dip

⅔ c. mayonnaise
1 c. sour cream
1 T. instant minced onion
1 T. parsley flakes
1 tsp. dill weed

Mix all ingredients. Serve with raw vegetables as allowed on your diet.

13 servings. Serving size: 2 T. Per serving: 121 calories, 13 g total fat (4 g saturated),
1 g protein, 1 g carbohydrate, 75 mg sodium, 38 mg potassium, 19 mg phosphorus.

Cassis Cooler

1 T. creme de cassis
½ t. lime juice
¾ c. club soda, chilled
Lime slices

Combine creme de cassis and lime juice in a wine glass; add club soda.
Stir and garnish with lime slice.

1 serving. Serving size: 3/4 cup. Per serving: 63 calories, 0 g total fat (0 g saturated),
0 g protein, 7 g carbohydrate, 38 mg sodium, 6 mg potassium, 0 mg phosphorus.

Champagne Punch

1 (6 oz.) can lemonade
1 lg. can pineapple juice
2 fifths white wine
1 fifth champagne
Ginger ale (optional)

Mix first 3 ingredients; add champagne (and ginger ale) to taste just
before serving. Add ice.

8 servings. Serving size: 1/2 cup. Per serving: 83 calories, 0 g total fat (0 g saturated),
0 g protein, 12 g carbohydrate, 4 mg sodium, 132 mg potassium, 12 mg phosphorus.

French 75's

1²/₃ c. brandy
¹/₄ c. lemon juice
¹/₄ c. corn syrup
1 fifth pink champagne, chilled
1 28 oz. bottle carbonated water, chilled

Combine brandy, lemon juice, and corn syrup; chill well. To serve, pour brandy mixture into chilled punch bowl. Slowly pour in champagne and carbonated water; stir gently. To serve, float frozen whole cranberries or seedless grapes in punch. Makes 9 cups.

18 servings. Serving size: 1/2 cup. Per serving: 68 calories, 0 g total fat (0 g saturated), 0 g protein, 4 g carbohydrate, 6 mg sodium, 12 mg potassium, 2 mg phosphorus.

Grape Mint Tea

1¹/₂ c. boiling water
3 lemon flavor tea bags
2 T. fresh mint
1 (24 oz.) bottle grape juice, chilled
1¹/₂ c. club soda, chilled

Combine water, tea, and mint, cover and steep about 7 minutes. Discard tea bags and mint; cover and chill. Add grape juice and club soda to tea just before serving. Pour over ice cubes, and garnish with fresh mint sprigs if desired.

12 servings. Serving size: 1/2 cup. Per serving: 43 calories, 0 g total fat (0 g saturated), 0 g protein, 0 g carbohydrate, 0 mg sodium, 33 mg potassium, 10 mg phosphorus.

Hawaiian Iced Tea

Make tea to taste and add mint for 3 min. To each 14 oz. add
   The juice of one-half lemon
   One tablespoon pineapple juice
   Three teaspoons sugar
Place in blender or cocktail shaker and mix well; chill. Before serving
add ice and a spear of fresh pineapple.

> 2 servings. Serving size: 1/2 cup. Per serving: 36 calories, 0 g total fat (0 g saturated),
> 0 g protein, 10 g carbohydrate, 0 mg sodium, 49 mg potassium, 3 mg phosphorus.

Holiday Champagne Punch

          4 cups cranberry juice
          4 cups pineapple juice
          1/2 c. lemon juice
          1 c. sugar
          1 bottle white wine
          2 bottles champagne

Combine cranberry, pineapple, and lemon juices. Add sugar and stir
until dissolved; chill. Add wine and mix well. Pour over ice in punch
bowl. Add champagne just before serving.

> 30 servings. Serving size: 1/2 cup. Per serving: 100 calories, 0 g total fat (0 g saturated),
> 0 g protein, 17 g carbohydrate, 4 mg sodium, 97 mg potassium, 9 mg phosphorus.

Hot Buttered Rum

1 quart apple juice
1/4 c. packed brown sugar
2 T. butter
Rum

Heat apple juice and brown sugar until mixture comes to a boil. Add butter. Pour into mugs. Add 1/2 jigger of rum to each half-cup serving.

8 servings. Serving size: 1/2 cup. Per serving: 117 calories, 3 g total fat (2 g saturated), 0 g protein, 19 g carbohydrate, 35 mg sodium, 164 mg potassium, 11 mg phosphorus.

Hot Cranberry Punch

2 1/2 c. pineapple juice
2 c. cranberry juice
1 3/4 c. water
3 (3") sticks cinnamon
1/4 c. packed brown sugar
1 T. whole cloves
1 1/2 tsp. whole allspice

Combine first 3 ingredients in water reservoir of a 10 cup electric coffeemaker. Place basket in glass carafe. Combine remaining ingredients in basket, omitting paper filter. Place spices in cheesecloth if desired. Cover coffeemaker with top. Brew mixture. Serve warm. Makes 6 cups.

13 servings. Serving size: 1/2 cup. Per serving: 61 calories, 0 g total fat (0 g saturated), 0 g protein, 15 g carbohydrate, 5 mg sodium, 85 mg potassium, 6 mg phosphorus.

Homemade Coffee Liqueur

Bring 3 cups water and 4 cups sugar to boil. Add split vanilla bean and boil 7 minutes. Blend in 1 cup instant coffee powder. Stirring constantly, add one fifth 100 proof vodka. Blend with wire whip and strain. Makes 2½ fifths.

32 servings. Serving size: 1/4 cup. Per serving: 121 calories, 0 g total fat (0 g saturated), 0 g protein, 26 g carbohydrate, 2 mg sodium, 64 mg potassium, 6 mg phosphorus.

Sparkling Cranberry Punch

2 qts. cranberry-apple juice
1 (6 oz.) can pink lemonade
1 qt. club soda, chilled

Combine thawed lemonade and cranberry-apple juice. Add soda before serving. Serve with an ice ring.

26 servings. Serving size: 1/2 cup. Per serving: 55 calories, 0 g total fat (0 g saturated), 0 g protein, 14 g carbohydrate, 9 mg sodium, 23 mg potassium, 3 mg phosphorus.

Sparkling Strawberry Punch

2 (10 oz.) pkg. frozen strawberries,
  slightly thawed
1 (6 oz.) can frozen lemonade,
  slightly thawed
1 fifth rose wine, chilled
2 (28 oz.) bottles ginger ale, chilled
1 (28 oz.) bottle club soda
$1/4$ to $1/2$ c. sugar

In covered blender container with blender at high speed, blend straw-berries and undiluted lemonade until well blended. Pour strawberry mixture into a chilled large punch bowl. Add wine and remaining ingredients; stir punch until sugar is completely dissolved. Serve over ice.

25 servings. Serving size: 1/2 cup. Per serving: 62 calories, 0 g total fat (0 g saturated), 0 g protein, 15 g. carbohydrate, 13 mg sodium, 46 mg potassium, 5 mg phosphorus.

Chapter 3

SALADS

Aloha Carrot Salad

3 med. carrots, shredded
1 sm. pkg. lemon gelatin
1 c. boiling water
½ c. cold water
1 (8 ¾ oz.) can crushed pineapple
(undrained)

Dissolve gelatin in boiling water. Add cold water and pineapple with liquid. Chill until slightly thickened. Fold in carrots. Pour into a 4-cup ring mold or 9 individual molds. Chill until firm.

9 servings. Serving size: 1/2 cup. Per serving: 63 calories, 2 g total fat (0 g saturated),
1 g protein, 15 g carbohydrate, 34 mg sodium, 112 mg potassium, 26 mg phosphorus.

Cauliflower–Green Bean Salad

1 med. head cauliflower
1 can unsalted cut green beans,
    drained
1 bottle low-sodium onion flavor
    salad dressing

Separate cauliflower and cook until just tender, about 10 min. Drain.
Put cauliflower and green beans in a bowl. Pour dressing over vegetables and toss. Chill overnight, stirring occasionally. Serve on lettuce.

9 servings. Serving size: 1/2 cup. Per serving: 29 calories, 1 g total fat (0 g saturated),
2 g protein, 5 g carbohydrate, 71 mg sodium, 178 mg potassium, 26 mg phosphorus.

Cherry–Berry Mold

1 env. unflavored gelatin
$1/4$ c. water
2 T. lemon juice
1 T. sugar
1 (12 oz.) can strawberry soda
    dark sweet cherries
$1/2$ c. sliced fresh or frozen
    strawberries

In a small saucepan soften gelatin in water. Cook and stir over low
heat until gelatin is dissolved. Add lemon juice and sugar; stir until
sugar is dissolved. Stir in strawberry soda; chill until partially set. Fold
in cherries and strawberries. Pour into a 3-cup mold. Chill until firm.

6 servings. Serving size: 1/2 cup. Per serving: 52 calories, 0 g total fat (0 g saturated),
1 g protein, 12 g carbohydrate, 15 mg sodium, 68 mg potassium, 6 mg phosphorus.

Chicken Salad

4 c. cooked chicken breast
¾ lb. green grapes
1 (16 oz.) can pineapple chunks
1 lg. apple, chopped
1½ c. mayonnaise
4 T. red wine vinegar
2 T. low-sodium soy sauce
½ c. minced onion
2 tsp. curry powder
1½ T. candied ginger
    (or 1 T. sugar) and ½ tsp.
    ginger)

Cube chicken and place in a large bowl. Add halved grapes, pineapple chunks, and chopped apple. In a separate bowl, combine remaining ingredients and let stand for 1 hour. Combine with chicken mixture. Chill for at least 1 hour.

18 servings. Serving size: 1/2 cup. Per serving: 199 calories, 15 g total fat (2 g saturated), 5 g protein, 11 g carbohydrate, 129 mg sodium, 137 mg potassium, 45 mg phosphorus.

Chicken Layer Salad

2 c. cubed, cooked chicken
$1/2$ tsp. curry powder
$1/4$ tsp. paprika
dash pepper
2 c. shredded lettuce
2 c. shredded romaine
1 c. shredded carrot
$1^{1}/2$ c. sliced cucumber
1 c. macaroni, cooked and drained
1 lg. green pepper, chopped
1 c. mayonnaise
2 T. milk
2 T. lemon juice
2 T. snipped parsley

In mixing bowl combine chicken, curry, paprika and pepper. Toss well. In a clear salad bowl, layer lettuce, romaine, coated chicken, cucumber, macaroni, and green pepper. Stir together mayonnaise, milk, lemon juice and a dash pepper. Spread over all. Cover; chill several hours or overnight. Sprinkle with parsley. Toss.

12 servings. Serving size: 3/4 cup. Per serving: 194 calories, 17 total fat (2 g saturated), 6 g protein, 7 g carbohydrate, 123 mg sodium, 164 mg potassium, 64 mg phosphorus.

Chilled Asparagus Salad

3 c. diagonally sliced asparagus
1 T. Balsamic vinegar
1 tsp. olive oil
1 T. minced parsley
1 tsp. minced garlic
2 T. lemon juice
Dash cayenne pepper
Fresh ground pepper

Blanch the asparagus in a pot of boiling water for 3 minutes; drain. Plunge into ice water and drain again. Whisk together the remaining ingredients and pour over asparagus. Refrigerate 1 hour before serving.

8 servings. Serving size: 1/2 c. Per serving: 27 calories, 1 g total fat (0 g saturated), 2 g protein, 4 g carbohydrate, 2 mg sodium, 196 mg potassium, 39 mg phosphorus.

Garden Salad

1 c. peeled and jullienned carrots
1 c. julienned green beans
1/2 c. frozen peas
1 c. julienned green zucchini
1 c. julienned yellow zucchini
1/2 c. chopped white onion
1/2 c. cored and julienned red sweet
    bell pepper

Dressing

2 T. chopped parsley
3/4 c. olive oil
2 T. white wine vinegar
Juice of 1 lemon
Freshly ground pepper to taste

In a large pot of simmering water, blanch the carrots, beans, and peas for a few minutes; drain and rinse immediately in cold water. Drain again. In a large bowl, toss the blanched vegetables with zucchini, onions, and red pepper. Mix together dressing ingredients; add to vegetables and toss well. Store, covered, in refrigerator until ready to serve.

13 servings. Serving size: 1/2 c. Per serving: 125 calories, 12 g fat (1 g saturated),
1 g protein, 3 g carbohydrates, 11 mg sodium, 131 mg potassium, 21 mg phosphorus.

Golden Apple Pasta Salad

6 oz. macaroni
$\frac{1}{2}$ c. salad oil
Lemon juice
2 T. white wine vinegar
2 tsp. Dijon mustard
1 tsp. sugar
$\frac{1}{4}$ tsp. pepper
$\frac{1}{2}$ c. chopped green onion
2 golden delicious apples,
    cored and sliced
$\frac{3}{4}$ c. cooked low-salt ham,
    chopped
$\frac{3}{4}$ c. cooked turkey, chopped
1 small zucchini, thinly sliced

Cook macaroni according to package directions. Combine oil, 3 T. lemon juice, vinegar, mustard and seasonings; mix well. Pour dressing over warm macaroni; refrigerate until completely cool. Reserve several apple slice for garnish; dip in lemon juice if desired. Dice remaining apples. Combine macaroni, diced apples, ham, turkey, zucchini, and green onion; chill several hours. Spoon salad into serving bowl. Arrange reserved apple slices on top.

10 servings. Serving size: 3/4 cup. Per serving: 200 calories, 12 g total fat (1 g saturated), 5 g protein, 19 g carbohydrate, 8 mg sodium, 193 mg potassium, 64 mg phosphorus.

Green Bean Salad

1½ lb. green beans, trimmed and
     cut into 2-inch widths
2½ T. plus 1 tsp. balsamic vinegar
1 tsp. Dijon mustard
1 tsp. minced garlic
Freshly ground pepper
4 T. extra-virgin olive oil
½ c. chopped green onion
1½ T. chopped parsley

Cook green beans in boiling water until tender. Meanwhile, whisk together vinegar, mustard, garlic and pepper to taste; add oil. Pour over green beans while they are still warm. Toss with green onions and parsley. Chill. Serve chilled or at room temperature.

9 servings. Serving size: 1/3 c. Per serving: 83 calories, 6 g total fat (1 g saturated), 1 g protein, 6 g carbohydrate, 20 mg sodium, 168 mg potassium, 31 mg phosphorus.

Honey Slaw

½ c. mayonnaise
2 T. vinegar
2 T. honey
¼ tsp. onion powder
¼ tsp. celery seed
6 c. shredded cabbage

Combine dressing ingredients and pour over cabbage. Mix well and refrigerate.

12 servings. Serving size: 1/2 cup. Per serving: 87 calories, 8 g total fat (2 g saturated), 1 g protein, 5 g carbohydrate, 59 mg sodium, 96 mg potassium, 11 mg phosphorus.

Hot Slaw Au Vin

3 c. thin-sliced cabbage
2 small onions, sliced
1 med. carrot, shredded
2 T. butter
1 T. sugar
¼ c. sherry wine
¼ c. Parmesan cheese

In a skillet melt butter over medium heat. Sauté vegetables 5 minutes. Add seasonings and sherry. Cover and cook for 10 minutes, stirring occasionally. Remove mixture to casserole dish, sprinkle with cheese and bake at 425 degrees until cheese melts, about 10 minutes.

12 servings. Serving size: 1/2 cup. Per serving: 48 calories, 3 g total fat (2 g saturated), 2 g protein, 5 g carbohydrate, 128 mg sodium, 88 mg potassium, 31 mg phosphorus.

Italian Tossed Salad

6 c. mixed greens
1 cup sliced radishes
1 small green pepper,
  cut into strips
1 c. shredded carrots
¼ c. grated Parmesan cheese
⅔ c. low-sodium Italian salad
  dressing

In a salad bowl combine lettuce, radishes, green pepper, carrot and cheese. Toss to mix. Cover and chill, if desired. Pour dressing over salad. Toss to coat.

10 servings. Serving size: 3/4 cup. Per serving: 43 calories, 2 g total fat (1 g saturated), 2 g protein, 5 g carbohydrate, 145 mg sodium, 174 mg potassium, 40 mg phosphorus.

Layered Salad

1 c. mayonnaise
1-2 T. vinegar
1 head lettuce, shredded
2-3 scallions, minced
1-2 large carrots, shredded
1 green pepper, chopped
1½ c. cooked peas, drained
3 tsp. sugar
Chopped parsley

Use a deep salad bowl or serving dish with straight sides. Plan on having 2 layers of each vegetable in the dish. In a small mixing bowl combine the mayonnaise with the vinegar; set aside. The consistency of the dressing should be thin enough to spread easily over the vegetable layers. In the salad bowl place a thin layer of each vegetable using about ½ the total amount. Over these first layers of vegetables, spread ½ the dressing and sprinkle 1½ tsp sugar on top. Again repeat the process using the rest of the vegetables, dressing and sugar. Sprinkle the parsley on top. Cover and chill several hours or overnight.

16 servings. Serving size: 1/2 cup. Per serving: 125 calories, 11 g total fat (2 g saturated), 2 g protein, 6 g carbohydrate, 86 mg sodium, 145 mg potassium, 34 mg phosphorus.

Lemon Cole Slaw

8 c. shredded cabbage
1 c. shredded carrots
1 small onion, minced
2 T. chopped parsley
1/3 c. sugar
1 1/2 tsp. celery seed
1 c. mayonnaise
1/2 c. fresh lemon juice

In large bowl combine cabbage, carrots, onion, and parsley. In small bowl combine sugar, celery seed, pepper, and mayonnaise. Stir with wire whisk, then gradually whisk in lemon juice. Pour over slaw, toss, cover and refrigerate.

20 servings. Serving size: 1/2 cup. Per serving: 105 calories, 9 g total fat (1 g saturated), 1 g protein, 7 g carbohydrate, 70 mg sodium, 108 mg potassium, 14 mg phosphorus.

Macaroni Salad

2 c. elbow macaroni
1/2 c. mayonnaise
1 T. lemon juice
1 tsp. sugar
1 large carrot, shredded
1 c. diced celery
1/4 c. finely chopped scallions
1/4 c. chopped green pepper
Pepper to taste
Salad greens

Cook macaroni according to package directions. Drain. Rinse with cold water and drain again.

Mix mayonnaise with lemon juice and sugar. Combine with macaroni and remaining ingredients, except greens. Chill. Serve on greens.

9 servings. Serving size 1/2 cup. Per serving: 141 calories, 10 g total fat (1 g saturated), 2 g protein, 11 g carbohydrate, 85 mg sodium, 93 mg potassium, 29 mg phosphorus.

Mandarin Orange Mold

2 pkg. (3 oz.) orange gelatin
1 pkg. (3 oz.) lemon gelatin
3 c. boiling water
1 1/2 c. cold water
1 can (20 oz.) crushed pineapple
2 cans (11 oz.) mandarin oranges,
     drained
1/2 - 3/4 sauterne or sherry

Dissolve gelatin in boiling water and add cold water. Cool and add remaining ingredients. Pour into 3 qt. mold and refrigerate. Stir mixture as it begins to jell so that fruit will not settle to bottom.

9 servings. Serving size: 1/2 cup. Per serving: 190 calories, 0 g total fat (0 g saturated), 3 g protein, 43 g carbohydrate, 81 mg sodium, 182 mg potassium, 52 mg phosphorus.

Oriental Cabbage Salad

1 (3 oz.) pkg. oriental noodle
     soup mix
4 c. shredded cabbage
4 green onions, sliced
2 T. sesame seed
3 T. vinegar
2 T. sugar
2 T. salad oil
1/2 tsp. white pepper
1/4 c. slivered almonds, tossed

Discard flavor packet from oriental soup mix. Crush noodles. In a large mixing bowl combine noodles, cabbage, onions, and sesame seed.

For dressing, in a screw top jar combine vinegar, sugar, oil and pepper; shake to mix well. Pour over cabbage mixture and toss. Cover and chill several hours or overnight. Before serving, stir in almonds.

12 servings. Serving size: 1/2 cup. Per serving: 81 calories, 5 g total fat (1 g saturated), 2 g protein, 9 g carbohydrate, 177 mg sodium, 97 mg potassium, 32 mg phosphorus.

Oriental Cabbage and Rice Salad

2 c. finely shredded Chinese
    cabbage
2 c. finely shredded red cabbage
2 c. cold, cooked Basmati rice,
    fluffed with a fork
1 c. cold, cooked wild rice, fluffed
    with a fork
1 c. coarsely shredded carrots
1 c. snow peas, lightly steamed
½ c. thinly sliced green onions
5 T. rice wine vinegar
1½ T. extra-virgin olive oil
1 T. water
1 T. low sodium soy sauce
1 tsp. sesame oil
1 tsp. minced garlic
1 tsp. minced fresh ginger

In a large bowl, combine the Chinese cabbage, red cabbage, Basmati
rice, wild rice, carrots, snow peas, and green onions. Toss lightly.
Combine remaining ingredients; add to salad and mix well.

12 servings. Serving size: 2/3 c. Per serving: 90 calories, 3 g total fat (1 g saturated),
2 g protein, 15 g carbohydrate, 58 mg sodium, 141 mg potassium, 31 mg phosphorus.

Pasta Crab Salad

6 oz. pasta, cooked and cooled
1 T. olive or salad oil
1 tsp. basil
1 T. chopped parsley
1 T. macadamia nuts, diced
1/4 tsp. minced garlic
2 oz. fresh or frozen crab
White pepper
2 T. low-salt poppy seed dressing

Heat oil and garlic, do not burn, let cool. Mix all ingredients together. Add white pepper to taste.

6 servings. Serving size: 2.5 oz. Per serving: 98 calories, 5 g total fat (1 g saturated), 3 g protein, 9 g carbohydrate, 70 mg sodium, 48 mg potassium, 61 mg phosphorus.

Pineapple Coleslaw

2 c. shredded red cabbage
2 c. shredded green cabbage
1-2 T. sugar
1 can (8 oz.) crushed pineapple
2 dashes nutmeg
2 dashes cinnamon
3/4 c. sour cream

Combine cabbages. Add sugar to crushed, undrained pineapple and simmer, uncovered, 5 minutes or until it becomes as thick as drained pineapple. Add spices and cool. Add cold sour cream and blend well. Chill. To serve, pour dressing over cabbage and toss to coat well.

12 servings. Serving size: 1/2 cup. Per serving: 56 calories, 3 g total fat (2 g saturated), 1 g protein, 7 g carbohydrate, 12 mg sodium 101 mg potassium, 19 mg phosphorus.

Pineapple Daiquiri Salad

½ c. cold pineapple syrup
2 envelopes unflavored gelatin
½ c. boiling pineapple syrup
½ c. light rum
1 (6 oz.) can frozen lemonade,
    thawed
2 c. ice cubes
1 (14 oz.) can crushed pineapple,
    well drained, reserve syrup

Put cold pineapple syrup and gelatin in blender container and process until gelatin is dissolved. Remove feeder cap and add boiling pineapple syrup. Add rum, limeade, and ice cubes. Pour into bowl, chill until slightly thickened. Fold in crushed pineapple. Pour into 6-cup mold and chill until firm. Unmold on serving plate and garnish with lime slices.

9 servings. Serving size: 1/2 cup. Per serving: 121 calories, 0 g total fat (0 g saturated), 1 g protein, 23 g carbohydrate, 4 mg sodium, 91 mg potassium 7 mg phosphorus.

Rice Salad With Shrimp

2 c. white rice
1/4 c. vegetable oil
1/3 c. white vinegar
1/4 tsp. pepper
1/4 tsp. dried tarragon
1/2 green pepper, minced
1/2 c. minced fresh parsley
1/2 c. minced scallions
1 c. cooked green peas
1/2 to 1 lb. cooked baby shrimp
Watercress sprigs

Cook and steam rice according to package directions. While rice is still hot, place in a large bowl and add the oil, vinegar, pepper and tarragon, tossing lightly to blend well. Cool to room temperature. Add green pepper, parsley, scallions, and peas, mixing in well. Cover and refrigerate for a minimum of 2 hours.

At serving time, pile the rice mixture on a chilled serving platter in the shape of a pyramid and garnish with the baby shrimp and watercress.

6 servings. Serving size: 3/4 cup. Per serving: 259 calories, 10 g total fat (1 g saturated), 15 g protein, 26 g carbohydrate, 132 mg sodium, 278 mg potassium, 142 mg phosphorus.

Summer Fruit Salad

2 c. red grape halves
1 c. shredded zucchini
1 c. shredded cabbage
1 med. apple, cut julienne style
1/2 c. low-sodium French dressing
1/2 c. shredded carrots

Combine ingredients; mix lightly. Chill.

12 servings. Serving size: 1/2 cup. Per serving: 56 calories, 2 g total fat (0 g saturated), 1 g protein, 9 g carbohydrate, 48 mg sodium, 119 mg potassium, 1 mg phosphorus.

Tuna Salad

⅓ c. mayonnaise
1 T. lemon juice
¼ tsp. dillweed
1 can low-sodium tuna
½ c. chopped cucumber,
   peeled and seeded
¼ c. chopped green onions

Stir together first 3 ingredients until smooth. Add drained tuna, cucumber, and green onion; toss until blended.

4 servings. Serving size: 1/4 cup. Per serving: 186 calories, 15 g total fat (2 g saturated), 12 g protein, 2 g carbohydrate, 125 mg sodium, 169 mg potassium, 83 mg phosphorus.

Tuna-Apple Salad

1/3 c. mayonnaise
Curry powder to taste
1 (6 oz.) can low-sodium tuna
1 med. apple, diced

Combine mayonnaise and curry powder. Add drained can of tuna and apple. Chill.

4 servings. Serving size: 1/4 cup. Per serving: 208 calories, 15 g total fat (2 g saturated), 13 g protein, 6 g carbohydrate, 125 mg sodium, 184 mg potassium, 87 mg phosphorus.

Vermicelli Salad

1 lb. vermicelli, cooked
8 oz. low-sodium Italian dressing

Marinate vermicelli in dressing for 24 hours in refrigerator. Add:

1 c. mayonnaise
2 T. salad oil
2 T. chopped green onions
3/4 c. chopped fresh parsley
1 tsp. oregano
1 tsp. basil
Garlic powder and lemon pepper
to taste

Cover and let sit in refrigerator another 12 hours. Add shrimp if desired before serving. Can be made a few days in advance.

16 servings. Serving size: 1/2 cup. Per serving: 172 calories, 14 g total fat (2 g saturated), 3 g protein, 22 g carbohydrate, 307 mg sodium, 75 mg potassium, 44 mg phosphorus.

Zesty Lime-Applesauce Mold

1 (16 oz.) can applesauce
1 sm. pkg. lime gelatin
1 c. carbonated lemon-lime soda

In saucepan combine applesauce and gelatin. Cook and stir until gelatin dissolves; cool to room temperature. Gently stir in lemon-lime soda. Turn into a 3½ c. mold. Chill until firm.

6 servings. Serving size: 1/2 cup. Per serving: 103 calories, 0 g total fat (0 g saturated), 2 g protein, 25 g carbohydrate, 42 mg sodium, 58 mg potassium, 25 mg phosphorus.

Cranberry-Apple Dressing

1 c. cranberry-apple juice
1 (3 oz.) pkg. liquid fruit pectin
1 (3") stick cinnamon
4 whole cloves
2 whole allspice

Combine juice and pectin in nonaluminum saucepan; stir well. Add remaining ingredients; bring to a boil, stirring constantly. Remove from heat; cover and chill 8 hours. Discard spices. Serve over apple or other fruit salad.

8 servings. Serving size: 2 T. Per serving: 68 calories, 0 g total fat (0 g saturated), 0 g protein, 18 g carbohydrate, 29 mg sodium, 9 mg potassium, 1 mg phosphorus.

Creamy Italian Dressing

2 T. tarragon vinegar
1 c. mayonnaise
1/2 small onion, cut up
1 T. sugar
3/4 tsp. Italian herbs
1/4 tsp. garlic powder
Dash pepper

Put all ingredients in blender and process until smooth. Chill until ready to serve. Yield: 1 1/4 c.

20 servings. Serving size: 1 T. Per serving: 83 calories, 9 g total fat (1 g saturated), 0 g protein, 1 g carbohydrate, 63 mg sodium, 9 mg potassium, 4 mg phosphorus.

French Dressing

½ c. sugar
½ tsp. paprika
Dash cayenne pepper
1 c. salad oil
½ c. vinegar
2 or 3 garlic cloves

Shake all ingredients together in a jar until sugar is dissolved. Continue to occasionally shake over a 24-hour period. Remove garlic before using. Yield: 1½ c.

24 servings. Serving size: 1 T. Per serving: 99 calories, 9 g total fat (1 g saturated), 0 g protein, 4 g carbohydrate, 0 mg sodium, 9 mg potassium, 1 mg phosphorus.

Herb French Dressing

¾ c. olive oil
2 T. vinegar
1 T. lemon juice
1 tsp. Dijon mustard
¼ tsp. pepper
1 T. chopped parsley
1 T. chopped chives
1 tsp. chervil

Combine all ingredients in a covered 1-quart jar and shake until well blended. Refrigerate dressing. Shake well before serving. Yield: 1 cup.

16 servings. Serving size: 1 T. Per serving: 91 calories, 10 g total fat (1 g saturated), 0 g protein, 0 g carbohydrate, 8 mg sodium, 8 mg potassium, 1 mg phosphorus.

Herb Mayonnaise

1 c. mayonnaise
1/2 T. lemon juice
1/4 tsp. paprika
1 tsp. basil
1 tsp. thyme
1 tsp. marjoram
1 T. minced onion
1 clove garlic, minced
1 T. chopped chives
1/8 tsp. curry powder
1/2 tsp. Worcestershire sauce
1/2 c. sour cream

Mix well and keep chilled. Use for chicken or tuna salad. Yield: 2 cups.

32 servings. Serving size: 1 T. Per serving: 58 calories, 6 g total fat (1 g saturated), 0 g protein, 1 g carbohydrate, 42 mg sodium, 14 mg potassium, 6 mg phosphorus.

Hot Cider Dressing

1 c. apple juice
1/2 c. sliced red onion
1/2 c. water
1/2 c. cider vinegar
2 T. brown sugar
1 T. cornstarch
2 tsp. poppy seeds
2 tsp. Dijon mustard

Combine apple juice and onion in nonaluminum saucepan; cook over medium heat 4 minutes or until onion is tender. Add remaining ingredients; stir well. Bring mixture to a boil over medium heat; cook 1 minute or until thickened, stirring constantly. Serve warm over salad greens. Yield: 1 1/2 cups

24 servings. Serving size: 1 T. Per serving: 13 calories, 0 g total fat (0 g saturated), 0 g protein, 3 g carbohydrate, 12 mg sodium, 28 mg potassium, 5 mg phosphorus.

Mediterranean Dressing

1 clove garlic, crushed
1/4 tsp. pepper
1/2 tsp. lemon rind
1/4 tsp. paprika
2 T. tarragon vinegar
1/2 c. olive oil
2 T. sour cream

In small mixing bowl combine the garlic, pepper, lemon rind, paprika and vinegar. Gradually add the olive oil, beating constantly with a wire whisk. When blended well, beat in the sour cream and mix thoroughly. Chill in refrigerator at least 2 hours before serving. Yield: 3/4 cup.

12 servings. Serving size: 1 T. Per serving: 85 calories, 9 g total fat (2 g saturated), 0 g protein, 0 g carbohydrate, 1 mg sodium, 8 mg potassium, 3 mg phosphorus.

Parsley Salad Dressing

3/4 c. olive oil
3 T. lemon juice
1/2 tsp. Dijon mustard
1/4 tsp. fresh ground pepper
1 c. minced fresh parsley
1 clove garlic, crushed

Place all the ingredients in blender. Blend at medium speed for 45 seconds. Chill. Yield: 1 cup.

16 servings. Serving size: 1 T. Per serving: 92 calories, 10 g total fat (1 g saturated), 0 g protein, 1 g carbohydrate, 6 mg sodium, 26 mg potassium, 3 mg phosphorus.

Poppy Seed Dressing

3/4 c. vegetable oil
1/3 c. lemon juice
1/2 c. sugar
1/4 small onion
1 tsp. dry mustard
1/2 tsp. grated lemon peel
1 T. poppy seed

Place first 6 ingredients in blender. Blend on high until well blended. Stir in poppy seeds. Chill. Yield: 1 1/2 cups.

24 servings. Serving size: 1 T. Per serving: 81 calories, 7 g total fat (1 g saturated), 0 g protein, 5 g carbohydrate, 0 mg sodium, 8 mg potassium, 4 mg phosphorus.

Sweet-Sour Dressing

3/4 c. sugar
1 c. salad oil
1/2 c. tarragon vinegar
1/2 tsp. paprika
1/2 tsp. onion juice
8 drops Worcestershire sauce

Place all ingredients in blender, and mix well. Chill. Yield: 2 cups.

32 servings. Serving size: 1 T. Per serving: 79 calories, 7 g total fat (0 g saturated), 0 g protein, 5 g carbohydrate, 3 mg sodium, 6 mg potassium, 0 mg phosphorus.

Vinaigrette Dressing

6 T. olive oil
1 clove garlic, mashed
2 T. wine vinegar
Juice of ½ lemon
1 tsp. fresh ground pepper

Place oil in bowl with garlic; stir well. Discard bits of garlic. Add remaining ingredients and beat well with wire whisk. Chill. Add additional seasonings to taste, such as basil, crushed red pepper, powdered mustard or chopped green onion. Yield: 1 cup.

16 servings. Serving size: 1 T. Per serving: 46 calories, 5 g total fat (1 g saturated), 0 g protein, 0 g carbohydrate, 0 mg sodium, 6 mg potassium, 1 mg phosphorus.

Chapter 4

BREADS AND SANDWICHES

Applesauce Loaf

1/2 c. margarine
1 c. sugar
2 eggs
1¾ c. sifted flour
1 tsp. baking powder
1/2 tsp. baking soda
1/2 tsp. cinnamon
1/2 tsp. nutmeg
1 c. applesauce

Glaze:

1/2 c. powdered sugar
1 T. water

Beat margarine and sugar until light. Add eggs, beat until light and fluffy. Sift together dry ingredients. Add to creamed mixture alternately with applesauce. Beat after each addition. Pour into a greased and floured loaf pan, 9 x 5 inches. Bake at 350 degrees for 1 hour. Cool in pan for 10 minutes. Remove to rack. Glaze: Mix sugar and water; brush on loaf.

12 servings. Serving size: 3/4" slice. Per serving: 236 calories, 9 g total fat (2 g saturated),
3 g protein, 38 g carbohydrate, 105 mg sodium, 49 mg potassium, 47 mg phosphorus.

61

Beef Tortillas

1 large carrot
½ small cucumber
1 3-oz. pkg. cream cheese with
    chives, softened
2 T. prepared white horseradish
1 T. milk
4 8-inch flour tortillas
Lettuce leaves
½ lb. thinly sliced cooked
    roast beef

Into small bowl, coarsely shred carrots and cucumber. In another small bowl, with spoon, mix cream cheese, horseradish and milk until blended. Spread horseradish mixture along center of tortillas. Top with lettuce leaves, then roast beef slices. Sprinkle with vegetables. Fold two opposite sides of each tortilla over filling, overlapping slightly.

8 servings. Serving size: 1/2 Tortilla. Per serving: 147 calories, 7 g total fat (3 g saturated), 10 g protein, 13 g carbohydrate, 139 mg sodium, 237 mg potassium, 102 mg phosphorus.

Garlic French Bread

Cut a 1 pound loaf of *French bread* horizontally in half. Mix 1/2 cup soft *margarine* with 1/4 tsp. *garlic powder*, spread mixture on cut sides of loaf. Reassemble loaf; cut crosswise into 1" slices. Wrap in foil. Heat 15 minutes at 350.

24 servings. Serving size: 1" slice. Per serving: 82 calories, 5 g total fat (5 g saturated), 1 g protein, 9 g carbohydrate, 107 mg sodium, 22 mg potassium, 19 mg phosphorus.

Herbed French Bread

1-1 lb. loaf French bread
½ c. sweet margarine or butter,
    softened
2 tsp. lemon juice
1 tsp. bouquet garni

Cut loaf of bread horizontally in half. Mix the butter with lemon juice
and bouquet garni. Spread mixture on cut sides of loaf. Reassemble
loaf; cut crosswise into 2" slices. Wrap in foil. Heat 15 minutes at 350
degrees.

24 servings. Serving size: 1" slice. Per serving: 82 calories, 5 g total fat (1 g saturated),
1 g protein, 9 g carbohydrate, 107 mg sodium, 22 mg potassium, 19 mg phosphorus.

Strawberry Bread

1 c. butter
11/2 c. sugar
1 tsp. vanilla
1/4 tsp. lemon extract
4 eggs
3 c. flour
1 tsp. baking powder
1 tsp. cream of tartar
1/2 c. sour cream
1 c. strawberry jam

Cream together butter, sugar, vanilla, and lemon extract until fluffy.
Add eggs, one at a time, beating well after each addition. Sift together
flour, baking powder, and cream of tartar. Mix together sour cream
and strawberry jam; add alternately with sifted dry ingredients to
creamed mixture, beating well. Bake in greased and floured loaf pans
at 350 degrees for 50 to 55 minutes. Cool in pans 10 minutes, removing to rack to cool completely. Make two 8 x 3 inch loaves, or five 4 x
2 inch loaves.

32 servings. Serving size: 1" slice. Per serving: 174 calories, 7 g total fat (5 g saturated),
2 g protein, 26 g carbohyrates, 85 mg sodium, 53 mg potassium, 32 mg phosphorus.

Lemon Muffins

1 c. butter
1 c. sugar
4 egg yolks, well beaten
2 c. flour
2 tsp. baking powder
½ c. lemon juice
4 egg whites
2 tsp. grated lemon rind

Cream butter and sugar. Add yolks, and beat until light. Add baking powder to flour, and alternating with lemon juice, add to yolk mixture. Do not overbeat. Beat whites until stiff but not dry, and fold into the batter with the lemon rind. Pour into greased muffin pans, filling each ¾ full. Bake at 375 degrees for 20 minutes. Yield: 2 dozen.

24 servings. Serving size: 1 muffin. Per serving: 153 calories, 9 g total fat (5 g saturated), 3 g protein, 17 g carbohydrate, 138 mg sodium, 37 mg potassium, 36 mg phosphorus.

Oven Pancake

½ c. flour
½ c. milk
2 eggs, lightly beaten
Pinch of nutmeg
4 T. butter
2 T. powdered sugar
Juice of ½ lemon

Combine flour, milk, eggs, and nutmeg. Beat lightly, leaving butter a little lumpy. Melt butter in a 12-inch oven-proof skillet. When butter is very hot, pour in batter. Bake in 425 degrees oven 15-20 minutes or until golden brown. Sprinkle with sugar and return briefly to oven. Sprinkle with lemon juice. Serve immediately with jam, jelly, marmalade, or maple syrup.

8 servings. Serving size: 1/8 pancake. Per serving: 108 calories, 7 g total fat (4 g saturated), 3 g protein, 9 g carbohydrate, 81 mg sodium, 54 mg potassium, 46 mg phosphorus.

Popovers

1 c. flour
1 T. sugar
1 T. butter, melted
1 c. milk
2 large eggs
Cooking oil

Combine all of the ingredients, except the oil, in blender for 45 seconds. Heat oil in tins and pour batter ⅔ full. Bake at 400 degrees for 40 minutes. Serve immediately with butter, jam or honey. Yield: 12 popovers.

12 servings. Serving size: 1 popover. Per serving: 70 calories, 2 g total fat (1 g saturated), 3 g protein, 10 g carbohydrate, 31 mg sodium, 56 mg potassium, 47 mg phosphorus.

Bean Sprout Chicken Sandwiches

1 c. chicken, cooked and
    finely chopped
¼ c. water chestnuts, chopped
2 T. parsley, snipped
2 tsp. low-sodium soy sauce
¼ c. mayonnaise
1 c. bean sprouts, drained
White bread slices

Combine chicken, water chestnuts, and parsley; mix well. Blend soy sauce and mayonnaise. Butter slices of bread, and spread with filling. Top with bean sprouts, and cover with remaining slices of bread.

4 servings. Serving size: 1/2 cup (w/o bread). Per serving: 145 calories, 12 g total fat (2 g saturated), 6 g protein, 4 g carbohydrate, 179 mg sodium, 140 mg potassium, 61 mg phosphorus.

Chicken Burgers

1 c. diced cooked chicken
½ c. dried bread crumbs
1 tsp. grated onion
⅛ tsp. pepper
2 egg whites
2 T. butter, softened
Hamburger buns
Lettuce leaves
Whole-berry cranberry sauce

In small bowl, mix first 5 ingredients, 1 T. butter and 1 T. water. Shape into desired number of patties. In 10-inch skillet over medium heat, melt 1 T. butter; add patties and cook about 10 minutes or until golden, turning once. Slice each bun horizontally in half. Serve patties in buns with lettuce and cranberry sauce.

4 servings. Serving size: 1 patty (w/o bun) Per serving: 136 calories, 7 g total fat (4 g saturated), 8 g protein, 9 g carbohydrate, 206 mg sodium, 97 mg potassium, 59 mg phosphorus.

Chicken On A Bun

3 large cloves garlic, skin on
1/4 c. mayonnaise
1 tsp. finely grated lemon zest
Freshly ground black pepper,
    to taste
2 small skinless and boneless
    chicken breasts
2 tsp. olive oil
4 T. fresh lemon juice
4 hamburger buns
8 lettuce leaves

Place garlic in small saucepan. Cover with water and bring to a boil. Reduce heat. Cook for 25 minutes. Drain; slip skins off. Mash and mix with mayonnaise, lemon zest and pepper. Refrigerate garlic-mayonnaise until read to use.

Preheat broiler. But chicken breasts in half lengthwise, removing center cartilage. Fan out the little fillet on the underside of each breast and lay flat on baking sheet. Brush each breast with oil; drizzle with lemon juice and sprinkle with pepper. Broil, 4 inches from heat, for 4 to 5 minutes, until cooked through but still moist.

Open buns and toast lightly. Spread both sides of buns with prepared garlic-mayonnaise. Lay a chicken breast on the bottom of each bun and top with lettuce.

4 servings. Serving size: 1 Filet (w/o bun) Per serving: 20 calories, 15 g total fat
(2 g saturated), 14 g protein, 3 g carbohydrate, 112 mg sodium, 201 mg potassium,
115 mg phosphorus.

Chopped Sirloin Sandwiches

White bread, toasted
1 lb. lean hamburger
1 tsp. Worcestershire
2 egg whites
2-3 t. chopped onion
Pepper

Mix the ingredients and spread on toasted bread, covering each slice completely. Broil until brown and bubbly. Serve immediately. Number of servings depends on individual dietary protein needs.

4 servings. Serving size: 4 oz. patty (w/o bun) Per serving: 237 calories, 14 g total fat (6 g saturated), 25 g protein, 1 g carbohydrate, 96 mg sodium, 268 mg potassium, 132 mg phosphorus.

Egg and Pepper Pita Sandwiches

1 T. margarine
1 small sliced onion
1 small sliced green pepper
1/4 tsp. basil
4 eggs, beaten
Pita pockets, halved
Lettuce leaves

Melt butter in medium skillet over medium heat. Add onion, green pepper and basil; cook, stirring, for 2-3 minutes. Add eggs, cook and stir until mixture is set. Line pitas with lettuce; spoon in egg mixture. Serve immediately.

4 servings. Serving size: 1/2 cup (w/o bread) Per serving: 109 calories, 7 g total fat (2 g saturated), 6 g protein, 5 g carbohydrate, 57 mg sodium, 145 mg potassium, 94 mg phosphorus.

Shredded Beef Sandwiches

1-3 lb. beef chuck roast
¼ c. vinegar
1 lg. onion, cut up
3 bay leaves
¼ tsp. ground cloves
⅛ tsp. garlic powder
Lettuce leaves
French rolls, split

Trim fat from roast. Cut roast, as necessary, to fit into a 3 or 4 quart electric slow cooker; place meat in cooker. Combine vinegar, onion, bay leaves, cloves, and garlic powder; pour over meat. Cover and cook on low heat setting for 11 to 12 hours or until meat is very tender. Remove meat and use two forks to shred meat; discard bones and fat. Line split rolls with lettuce leaves. Place shredded beef on rolls. Strain meat juices; skim off fat. Serve juices with sandwiches for dipping.

12 servings. Serving size: 4 oz. Per serving: 174 calories, 6 g total fat (2 g saturated), 26 g protein, 2 g carbohydrate, 51 mg sodium, 251 mg potassium, 212 mg phosphorus.

Stroganoff Steak Sandwiches

$2/3$ c. beer
$1/3$ c. cooking oil
$1/4$ tsp. garlic powder
$1/4$ tsp. pepper
2 T. butter or margarine
$1/4$ tsp. paprika
4 c. sliced onions
French bread slices, toasted
1 c. sour cream, warmed
$1/2$ tsp. prepared horseradish
2 lb. flank steak

In shallow dish combine first 4 ingredients. Marinate flank steak overnight in refrigerator; drain. Broil steak 3″ from heat for 5 to 7 minutes on each side. In saucepan, melt butter, blend in paprika. Cook onion until tender. Thinly slice meat across grain. Arrange meat on bread; top with onions. Combine sour cream and horseradish. Spoon a dollop on top of each sandwich.

16 servings. Serving size: 2 oz. (w/o bread) Per serving: 189 calories, 14 g total fat (5 g saturated), 18 g protein, 1 g carbohydrate, 60 mg sodium, 252 mg potassium, 127 mg phosphorus.

Shrimp Puffs

¼ lb. bay shrimp, cooked
4 water chestnuts, minced
1 green onion, minced
2 egg whites, beaten
4 slices white bread
¼ tsp. ginger
Freshly ground pepper
4 T. sour cream
1 T. lemon juice

Remove crusts from bread and toast until crisp. Combine remaining ingredients and stir until well mixed. Spread mixture on prepared bread slices. Cut each slice into fourths (squares, triangles, or long fingers). Place shapes on a cookie sheet and broil until puffy and golden.

16 servings. Serving size: 1 piece. Per serving: 39 calories, 1 g total fat (1 g saturated), 3 g protein, 4 g carbohydrate, 57 mg sodium, 42 mg potassium, 28 mg phosphorus.

Shrimp-Topped Rice Cakes

3 c. water
$^3/_4$ lb. medium-size fresh shrimp
1 (8 oz.) pkg. cream cheese,
    softened
2 T. chopped fresh chives
$^1/_8$ tsp. red pepper
Plain rice cakes

Bring 3 cups water to a boil; add shrimp and cook 3 to 5 minutes. Drain well, rinse under cold, running water. Chill. Peel and devein shrimp; chop.

Combine cheese, chives, and pepper in a small bowl; beat at medium speed of an electric mixer until smooth. Stir in shrimp and blend mixture well.

Spread $^1/_4$ cup mixture on each rice cake; place rice cakes on a baking sheet. Broil 5 to 6 inches from heat 2 to 5 minutes or until warm. Serve immediately.

8 servings. Serving size: 1/4 cup (w/o rice cake) Per serving: 145 calories, 11 g total fat
(6 g saturated), 11 g protein, 1 g carbohydrate, 150 mg sodium, 115 mg potassium,
117 mg phosphorus.

Herbed Melba Toast

1 loaf thin-cut bread
½ c. butter, softened
1 small clove garlic, mashed
1 T. minced parsley
¼ tsp. basil
¼ tsp. oregano
Few grains pepper
Sesame seeds

Remove crusts from the bread, and cut each slice into 3 equal pieces. Combine butter, garlic, parsley, basil, oregano, and pepper. Spread on bread, and sprinkle with sesame seeds. Bake in 325 degree oven for about 7 minutes or until toasted. Yield: 75 pieces.

15 servings. Serving size: 5 pieces. Per serving: 96 calories, 7 g total fat (4 g saturated), 1 g protein, 7 g carbohydrate, 134 mg sodium, 23 mg potassium, 20 mg phosphorus.

Sesame Herb Toast or Bread

¼ lb. butter
2 T. sesame seeds
1/4 tsp. marjoram
1 T. chopped chives
¼ tsp. basil
¼ tsp. rosemary

Soften butter, mix with rest of ingredients and spread on bread. You can either put on bread slices and toast under boiler, or cut French bread diagonally and put on butter and wrap in foil and heat at 325 degrees for 15 minutes.

8 servings. Serving size: 1 T. Per serving: 115 calories, 12 g total fat (7 g saturated), 1 g protein, 1 g carbohydrate, 118 mg sodium, 18 mg potassium, 18 mg phosphorus.

Chapter 5

MEATS

Beef, Cabbage and Rice

2 T. vegetable oil
3 c. cooked rice, chilled
3/4 lb. lean top round
1 T. low-salt soy sauce
1/2 tsp. black pepper
1/2 c. thinly sliced onions
1/2 c. sliced green pepper
1 1/2 c. shredded Chinese cabbage
   (won bok)

Heat 1 T. oil in skillet; sauté and stir rice 5 minutes. Keep warm. Cut beef in thin strips and toss with soy sauce. Heat remaining oil; add undrained beef; cook 1 minute over high heat, stirring steadily. Add onions, green pepper, cabbage, and pepper. Cook on medium heat 5 minutes. Serve beef mixture over warmed rice.

8 servings. Per serving: 195 calories, 5 g total fat (1 g saturated), 12 g protein, 24 g carbohydrate, 92 mg sodium, 221 mg potassium, 115 mg phosphorus.

Beef Chofleur

1 lb. boneless round steak
1 small head cauliflower
2 T. butter or margarine
1 green pepper, sliced
2 T. low-salt soy sauce
1 clove garlic, minced
2 T. cornstarch
½ tsp. sugar
1½ c. salt-free beef broth
1 c. sliced green onions
3 c. hot cooked rice

Cut meat into ½ inch cubes. Separate the cauliflower into flowerettes. Brown meat in butter about 5 minutes; add cauliflower, green pepper, soy sauce, and garlic. Stir lightly to coat vegetables with soy. Cover pan and simmer until vegetables are barely tender, about 10 minutes. Blend cornstarch, sugar and beef broth; add to meat mixture with green onions. Cook, stirring constantly, until thoroughly heated and sauce is thickened. Serve over rice.

8 servings. Per serving: 258 calories, 9 g total fat (4 g saturated), 15 g protein, 28 g carbohydrate, 204 mg sodium, 354 mg potassium, 136 mg phosphorus.

Beef with Vegetables

1 lb. green beans
½ lb. flank steak
2 tsp. cornstarch
1 tsp. sugar
1 tsp. low-salt soy sauce
1 tsp. salad oil
2 T. salad oil
1 green onion, sliced
1 cup beef stock
¼ c. water
1 T. cornstarch
½ tsp. low-salt soy sauce

Cook green beans until slightly tender. Slice meat ⅛″ thick against the grain in 2″ strips. Combine 2 tsp. cornstarch, sugar, soy sauce, and 1 tsp. salad oil. Add beef and toss lightly. Sauté in 1 T. oil over high heat until meat is cooked (about 5 minutes). Remove meat and clean pan with a paper towel. Add remaining oil and sauté green beans and onion stirring constantly (about 2 minutes). Add beef stock and bring to a boil. Blend cornstarch, water and ½ tsp. soy sauce. Add to the hot mixture and cook, stirring constantly, until slightly thickened (about 5 minutes). Add the meat, and serve over rice.

8 servings. Per serving: 112 calories, 6 g total fat (1 g saturated), 8 g protein,
6 g carbohydrate, 67 mg sodium, 285 mg potassium, 74 mg phosphorus.

Chinese Beef and Asparagus

1 tsp. cornstarch
2 T. low-salt soy sauce
$\frac{1}{2}$ lb. beef, sliced
4 T. oil
1 T. cornstarch
$\frac{1}{2}$ c. sugar
$\frac{1}{3}$ c. vinegar
4 T. water
1$\frac{1}{2}$ c. chopped asparagus
$\frac{1}{4}$ c. chopped green onions

Combine cornstarch and soy. Add to beef and mix well. Heat pan and add oil. Add mixture of cornstarch, sugar, vinegar, and water and bring to a boil. Add asparagus and simmer until tender. Stir in beef and marinade and simmer briefly, about 3 seconds. Add green onions and stir 1 second.

6 servings. Per serving: 228 calories, 12 g total fat (2 g saturated), 10 g protein, 22 g carbohydrate, 189 mg sodium, 237 mg potassium, 91 mg phosphorus.

Curried Beef

1 lb. chuck, cubed
2 c. water
2 T. oil
1 lg. onion, chopped
1 T. curry powder
1 T. chili powder
1 tsp. ground cumin
½ tsp. dry mustard
4 whole cloves
2 T. catsup
1 apple, chopped

Brown chuck in large skillet. Add water; simmer 1 hour. Drain, reserving broth. Sauté onion in oil until tender, but not brown. Add reserved broth, spices, and catsup. Simmer for 5 minutes. Add meat and simmer 10 minutes. Add apple and simmer 15 minutes more. Sauce should be fairly thick. Correct with more broth if too thick.

8 servings. Per serving: 170 calories, 8 g total fat (3 g saturated), 17 g protein, 9 g carbohydrate, 56 mg sodium, 279 mg potassium, 142 mg phosphorus.

Flemish Beef

3 lb. chuck or round beef
3 T. oil
2 c. sliced onions
½ tsp. ground pepper
⅛ tsp. thyme
1½ c. beer
1 T. sugar
1 T. vinegar

Trim all fat from beef; cut into 2-inch cubes. Heat the oil in Dutch oven or heavy saucepan; brown the onions and beef in it. Add the peppers, thyme, beef, sugar, and vinegar. Cover and cook over low heat 1½ hours or until meat is tender: Skim the fat.

15 servings. Per serving: 166 calories, 6 g total fat (2 g saturated), 21 g protein, 3 g carbohydrate, 45 mg sodium, 308 mg potassium, 166 mg phosphorus.

Italian Beef

3 lb. rump roast
1 stalk celery, diced
1 med. onion, chopped
1 tsp. garlic powder
Ground pepper
1 bay leaf
2 t. low-salt soy sauce
2 med. green peppers, parboiled

Cover roast with water and bring to a boil. Add all remaining ingredients and simmer 3 hours. Cool overnight for best results. Slice thin, and put in shallow pan in layers. Pour juice over meat; add more garlic powder and soy sauce. Slice green peppers over meat; heat 15 minutes in slow oven.

12 servings. Per serving: 203 calories, 11 g total fat (4 g saturated), 22 g protein, 2 g carbohydrate, 69 mg sodium, 261 mg potassium, 193 mg phosphorus.

Italian Meatballs

1lb. lean ground beef
1 slice bread, trimmed
1/4 c. milk
2 tsp. grated lemon rind
1/4 tsp. freshly ground pepper
2 egg whites
3 T. flour
2 T. vegetable oil

Soak bread in milk; drain and mash smooth. Mix together meat, bread, lemon rind, pepper, and egg. Sprinkle the flour onto a board and form cakes 1/2 inch thick and 1 inch in diameter. Heat oil in skillet; brown cakes for 2 minutes per side.

6 servings. Per serving: 227 calories, 14 g total fat (4 g saturated), 17 g protein, 6 g carbohydrate, 84 mg sodium, 191 mg potassium, 105 mg phosphorus.

Sweet and Sour Meatballs

2 lb. ground beef, prepared as
   meatballs in usual manner
1/2 c. water
2 1/2 c. pineapple chunks
1/4 c. brown sugar
2 T. cornstarch
1/4 c. white vinegar
3 T. low-salt soy sauce
1 green pepper, sliced
2 onions, thinly sliced

Sauté prepared meatballs in small amount of shortening. Add water, simmer 20 minutes. Drain pineapple, reserve liquid. Combine sugar and cornstarch, add pineapple syrup, vinegar, and soy. Add mixture to meatballs, cook until gravy thickens. Add pineapple, green pepper, and onion. Cook 5 minutes. Serve with hot white rice.

8 servings. Per serving: 295 calories, 15 g total fat (6 g saturated), 24 g protein,
17 g carbohydrate, 248 mg sodium, 361 mg potassium, 142 mg phosphorus.

Honey Tarragon Ribs

3 to 4 lobs. beef short ribs
1 c. dry white wine
$1/3$ c. white wine vinegar
1 lg. onion, chopped
1 clove minced garlic
2 T. dry mustard
$1/2$ tsp. dried tarragon
$1/4$ c. honey

In a 5 to 6-quart pan, combine short ribs, wine, vinegar, onion, garlic, mustard, tarragon, and honey. Cover and simmer, turning meat occasionally, until meat is very tender when pierced, about 2 hours. Skim off fat. Remove ribs and place on rack in a 12 x 15-inch broiler pan and broil about 6 inches from heat. Turn often, browning all sides, 8 to 10 minutes. Boil pan drippings, uncovered, until reduced to 1 cup. Serve with ribs.

8 servings. Per serving: 257 calories, 12 g total fat (5 g saturated), 20 g protein, 12 g carbohydrate, 37 mg sodium, 254 mg potassium, 147 mg phosphorus.

BBQ Pot Roast

1 chuck roast, 2″ thick
     (about $2^{1}/2$ lbs.)
$1/4$ c. low-salt soy sauce
$1/4$ c. water
1 T. lemon juice
$1/4$ c. bourbon or brandy
1 tsp. Worcestershire sauce
$1/4$ c. packed brown sugar

Place meat in a large shallow nonmetal dish. Combine remaining ingredients and pour over meat. Cover and refrigerate for at least 6 hours, turning meat once. Grill 5 inches from hot coals for 10 to 12 minutes on each side for rare, spooning marinade over meat each time it is turned. To serve, slice on the diagonal.

10 servings. Per serving: 305 calories, 20 g total fat (8 g saturated), 22 g protein, 6 g carbohydrate, 255 mg sodium, 296 mg potassium, 174 mg phosphorus.

German Pot Roast

3½ lb. pot roast
1 onion, sliced
6 whole cloves
Piece of ginger root
small piece of cinnamon stick
1 can beer
2 T. oil

Put beef with other ingredients (except oil) in large pan and marinate overnight in refrigerator. Wipe meat dry and brown slowly in oil. Add marinade, cover and simmer for 3 hours or until tender. Serve with pan juices.

12 servings. Per serving: 223 calories, 10 g total fat (3 g saturated), 27 g protein, 2 g carbohydrate, 46 mg sodium, 286 mg potassium, 237 mg phosphorus.

Sauerbraten

3 lb. round or rump beef
2 c. cider vinegar
2 tsp. sugar
3 cloves
8 peppercorns
1 c. chopped onion
1 c. sliced carrots
2 bay leaves
2 T. oil
½ c. boiling water

Trim fat from roast. Place in glass or pottery bowl. Bring to a boil the vinegar, sugar, cloves, peppercorns, onions, carrots, and bay leaves. Pour over meat; cover and marinate in the refrigerator 2-3 days, turning the meat several times. Drain, reserving all the vegetables and 1 cup liquid. Dry the meat. Heat oil in a Dutch oven or heavy saucepan; brown the meat in it. Pour off any fat. Heat the marinade and add to the meat with the water. Cover and cook over low heat for 2½ hours or until tender. Thicken gravy with 2 tsp. flour mixed with 1 T. water, if necessary.

12 servings. Per serving: 236 calories, 14 g total fat (4 g saturated), 2 g protein, 6 g carbohydrate, 43 mg sodium, 299 mg potassium, 196 mg phosphorus.

Skewered Marinated Mixed Grill

1 lb. flank steak
1 lb. boned, skinned chicken
   breast
½ c. lime juice
2 T. olive oil
4 cloves garlic, minced
1 tsp. red pepper flakes
Vegetable cooking spray

Partially freeze steak; trim fat from steak, and cut diagonally across grain into ¼-inch thick slices. Thread steak onto 8 (12-inch) wooden skewers. Cut chicken into 1-inch wide strips; thread onto 8 (12-inch) skewers. Place beef skewers in a shallow, nonmetal dish; place chicken skewers in another shallow, nonmetal dish. Combine lime juice, oil, garlic, and pepper in a small bowl; stir well. Pour half of mixture over beef skewers and remaining mixture over chicken. Cover and refrigerate 8 hours, turning occasionally. Remove skewers from marinade, reserving marinade. Coat grill rack with cooking spray, and place on grill over medium-hot coals; place skewers on rack. Cook beef skewers 2 minutes on each side or until desired degree of doneness; cook chicken skewers 3 minutes on each side or until done, basting beef and chicken occasionally with reserved marinade.

8 servings. Per serving: 191 calories, 9 g total fat (3 g saturated), 25 g protein, 2 g carbohydrate, 74 mg sodium, 348 mg potassium, 217 mg phosphorus.

Flank Steak with Lemon and Parsley

1 flank steak (1¼ lb.),
    well trimmed
4 tsp. olive oil
1 T. fresh lemon juice
Freshly ground pepper
1 T. chopped fresh parsley
1 tsp. chopped garlic
¼ tsp. grated lemon peel

Preheat broiler. Sprinkle both sides of steak with pepper. Broil 5 inches from heat 4 to 5 minutes per side for medium rare. Transfer to carving board. Cover and let stand 5 minutes.

Meanwhile, whisk oil, lemon juice, parsley, garlic, lemon peel, and 1/4 tsp. pepper in small bowl. Slice steak diagonally against the grain. Transfer to platter; pour on lemon dressing.

6 servings. Per serving: 196 calories, 11 g total fat (4 g saturated), 22 g protein,
1 g carbohydrate, 67 mg sodium, 344 mg potassium, 193 mg phosphorus.

Perfect BBQ Steak

2½ to 3 lb. top sirloin steak,
2″ thick,
1½ T. lemon pepper
4 T. butter
1 clove garlic, halved
½ tsp. Worcestershire sauce

Trim the steak, leaving about ¼-inch fat around the sides. The steak must be at room temperature. Sprinkle on both sides with the lemon pepper and rub in well. Have the barbecue coals flaming hot before cooking. Place the steak on the grill 2-3 inches from coals. Grill 6-8 minutes per side. The steak will flame and char, sealing in juices. Place the grilled meat on a warm, ovenproof platter and place in a preheated 300 degree oven for 15 minutes. Remove the meat and turn the oven to 250 degrees. Rub both sides of the meat with the cut garlic clove and smear both sides with 3 T. of the butter. Place the remaining 1 T. butter on top of the meat and sprinkle with the Worcestershire. Return to the oven for 10 minutes. Remove from oven and let sit for 4-5 minutes before carving. Slice in thin strips and arrange strips on the platter, pouring pan juices over top.

10 servings. Per serving: 187 calories, 10 g total fat (5 g saturated), 22 g protein,
1 g carbohydrate, 272 mg sodium, 296 potassium, 174 mg phosphorus.

Tenderloin Deluxe

2 T. softened butter
2 lb. beef tenderloin
2 T. butter
1/4 c. chopped green onion
2 T. low-salt soy sauce
1 tsp. Dijon mustard
dash freshly ground pepper
3/4 c. sherry

Spread softened butter on tenderloin and place on foil-lined baking pan. Bake uncovered at 400 degrees for 20 minutes. In a saucepan, melt 2 T. butter and sauté green onion until tender. Add soy sauce, mustard, pepper, and sherry and heat until boiling. Pour sauce over meat and bake an additional 20–25 minutes. Baste frequently with sauce from pan.

8 servings. Per serving: 265 calories, 14 g total fat (7 g saturated), 24 g protein, 3 g carbohydrate, 256 mg sodium, 382 mg potassium, 205 mg phosphorus.

VEAL

BBQ Indian Veal

1 c. olive oil
¼ c. lemon juice
¼ c. white wine vinegar
2 T. curry powder
2 cloves crushed garlic
2 tsp. turmeric
1 (4 lb.) filet roast of veal
1 lemon, thinly sliced
8-10 springs parsley

In a medium sized bowl mix together the oil, lemon juice, vinegar, curry, garlic, and turmeric. Marinate the veal in a shallow dish for at least 3 hours, turning the meat occasionally. To barbecue, cook the meat 6-8 inches from medium-hot coals for about 5–6 minutes per side or until brown on the outside. The inside should be pale pink, almost white. Place on a small warmed platter and garnish with the lemon slices and parsley sprigs. Cut in slices and serve.

16 servings. Per serving: 261 calories, 19 g total fat (4 g saturated), 21 g protein, 2 g carbohydrate, 69 mg sodium, 326 mg potassium, 191 mg phosphorus.

Gourmet Veal

3 T. butter
6 veal cutlets, ½″ thick
Fresh ground pepper
1 T. flour
1 c. meat stock mixed with
　4 tsp. Coinstreau®
3 lemons, sliced thin

Melt butter, seasoned cutlets with pepper, and cook until brown. Remove meat from pan and keep warm on hot platter. Sprinkle flour on remaining butter in pan and stir over heat until slightly brown. Warm meat stock and Cointreau; pour over mixture in pan. Stir 1 minute over low heat. Arrange veal on hot platter, cover with sauce. Garnish with lemon.

> 6 servings. Per serving: 295 calories, 20 g total fat (9 g saturated), 25 g protein,
> 4 g carbohydrate, 135 mg sodium, 300 mg potassium, 184 mg phosphorus.

Herbed Veal Kabobs

1 lb. veal leg cutlets, cut ¼ inch
　thick
4 green onions, sliced diagonally
　into 1½ inch pieces
2 T. olive oil
½ tsp. dried thyme, crushed
1 large clove garlic, crushed
¼ tsp. pepper

Combine olive oil and seasoning ingredients in 1 c. glass measure; heat in microwave on high for 45 seconds or until warm; set aside.

Cut veal into 1-inch wide strips. Alternately thread veal and green onion pieces on skewers. Brush both sides of kabobs with reserved seasoning mix. Place kabobs on grill over medium coals. Grill 4 to 5 minutes, turning once.

> 4 servings. Per serving: 228 calories, 17 g total fat (5 g saturated), 18 g protein,
> 2 g carbohydrate, 48 mg sodium, 211 mg potassium, 133 mg phosphorus.

Piquant Veal

1 c. dry bread crumbs
1 clove minced garlic
1 tsp. dry mustard
2 T. minced parsley
1 lb. veal scallops
3/4 c. dry white wine
2 T. oil
1/2 tsp. Worcestershire sauce
2 drops Tabasco® sauce

Mix together the bread crumbs, garlic, mustard and parsley. Dip the scallops in the wine (reserve any remaining wine) and then into crumb mixture. Heat the oil in a skillet, sauté the scallops until brown on both sides and tender. Transfer to a heated serving dish. Stir the Worcestershire sauce, Tabasco and remaining wine into the skillet, scraping the bottom and sides well. Bring to a boil and pour over veal.

6 servings. Per serving: 263 calories, 11 g total fat (2 g saturated), 22 g protein,
13 g carbohydrate, 201 mg sodium, 243 potassium, 168 mg phosphorus.

Sherried Veal Scallops

1 lb. veal scallops
6 T. milk
1/4 c. flour
2 T. butter or margarine
1/4 tsp. white pepper
1/3 c. sweet sherry
1 T. minced parsley

Dip the scallops in milk then in flour. Melt the butter in skillet; sauté the scallops until browned well on both sides and tender. Transfer to a heated serving dish; sprinkle with pepper. Stir the sherry into skillet, scraping bottom and sides. Bring to a boil and pour over scallops. Sprinkle with the parsley.

6 servings. Per serving: 211 calories, 9 g total fat (4 g saturated), 21 g protein,
6 g carbohydrate, 98 mg sodium, 222 mg potassium, 164 mg phosphorus.

Veal Piccata

1 lb. veal scallops
¼ c. flour
¼ tsp. pepper
3 T. oil
3 T. lemon juice
2 T. minced parsley

Pound veal as thin as possible between 2 pieces of waxed paper. Dip the veal in a mixture of the flour and pepper. Heat oil in a skillet; sauté veal until browned on both sides and tender. Remove veal and keep warm. Stir the lemon juice and parsley into skillet; cook 30 seconds, scraping pan of any browned particles. Pour over veal.

6 servings. Per serving: 215 calories, 12 g total fat (2 g saturated), 21 g protein,
5 g carbohydrate, 51 mg sodium, 198 mg potassium, 147 mg phosphorus.

Veal Scallopine

4 veal cutlets
1 clove garlic, quartered
2 T. oil
1 T. flour
freshly ground pepper
¼ tsp. nutmeg
1 sm. onion, thinly sliced
½ c. sherry or marsala wine
½ tsp. paprika
2 t. chopped parsley

Sauté garlic in oil over low heat for 5 minutes. Discard garlic. Brown cutlets in oil. Mix flour, pepper, and nutmeg. Sprinkle over browned meat. Add onion and wine. Cover skillet and simmer about 20 minutes, turning the meat several times. Add more wine if necessary. Serve on a warm platter with the sauce, garnished with paprika and parsley.

5 servings. Per serving: 255 calories, 17 g total fat (5 g saturated), 20 g protein,
2 g carbohydrate, 55 mg sodium, 240 mg potassium, 152 mg phosphorus.

Veal Scallopine with Zucchini

1 lb. veal cutlets
2 T. flour
$\frac{1}{2}$ tsp. basil
$\frac{1}{8}$ tsp. pepper
Vegetable cooking spray
1 T. olive oil
1 med. zucchini, sliced thin
1 clove minced garlic
1 T. lemon juice
1 T. water
1 tsp. capers

Trim fat from cutlets. Flatten to $\frac{1}{8}$ inch between 2 sheets of waxed paper with meat mallet. Combine flour, basil, and pepper; dredge cutlets in this mixture. Coat a large skillet with cooking spray; add oil. Place over medium-high heat until hot. Cook veal 4–5 minutes per side. Drain on paper towels, reserving drippings in pan. Transfer veal to serving platter; keep warm. Add zucchini and garlic to skillet; cook 2 minutes, stirring until tender. Spoon mixture over veal. Add lemon juice and water to skillet, bring to a boil, scraping brown bits from bottom of pan. Stir in capers. Spoon over veal.

5 servings. Per serving: 249 calories, 15 g total fat (5 g saturated), 22 g protein, 4 g carbohydrate, 122 mg sodium, 310 mg potassium, 174 mg phosphorus.

Balsamic Pork Chops

2 tsp. olive oil
4 pork chops 1 inch thick (1½ lb.)
Freshly ground pepper
½ c. minced shallots
½ c. no-salt-added chicken broth
¼ c. Balsamic vinegar
¼ tsp. dried thyme
1 T. butter

Heat oil in skillet over medium-high heat just until smoking. Sprinkle chops with pepper. Add chops to skillet and cook 5 minutes per side. Transfer to platter and keep warm.

Add shallots to pan; cook, stirring 1 minute. Add broth, vinegar and thyme; cook, stirring over high heat 5 minutes; remove from heat, stir in butter. Pour over chops.

4 servings. Per serving: 314 calories, 21 g total fat (7 g saturated), 25 g protein,
7 g carbohydrate, 109 mg sodium, 495 mg potassium, 248 mg phosphorus.

Honey Mustard Pork

1 lb. pork tenderloin
¼ c. honey
2 T. brown sugar
2 T. white or cider vinegar
1 T. Dijon mustard
¼ tsp. ground ginger

Combine honey, brown sugar, vinegar, mustard, and ginger; spread over pork. Roast in preheated 375 degree oven for 20 to 30 minutes until meat thermometer registers 160 degrees. Remove from oven and let stand 5 minutes before slicing.

4 servings. Per serving: 218 calories, 6 g total fat (2 g saturated), 18 g protein,
23 g carbohydrate, 129 mg sodium, 289 mg potassium, 126 mg phosphorus.

PORK

Luau Pork Chops

6 pork loin chops (½″)
1 (20 oz.) can pineapple slices
   in juice
Water
¼ c. brown sugar
3 T. low-salt soy sauce
2 T. dry sherry
½ tsp. ground ginger
¼ tsp. pepper

Trim several pieces of fat from edge of port chops. In 12-inch skillet over medium-high heat, heat fat until lightly browned; using spoon, press and rub fat over bottom of skillet to grease it well; discard fat. Add 3 chops to skillet; over high heat, cook until well browned on both sides, removing chops from skillet as they brown. Repeat with remaining chops.

Meanwhile, info measuring cup, drain pineapple juice; add water to make 1 cup. Reserve pineapple slices. Return chops to skillet; add pineapple-juice mixture, brown sugar, soy sauce, sherry, ginger, and pepper; heat to boiling. Reduce heat to low, cover and simmer 35 minutes or until chops are fork tender, turning once. Add pineapple; cook 5 minutes.

6 servings. Per serving: 327 calories, 15 g total fat (5 g saturated), 25 g protein, 22 g carbohydrate, 316 mg sodium, 568 mg potassium, 11242 phosphorus.

Oriental Pork Chops

6 pork loin chops (½")
¼ tsp. pepper
½ c. water
½ tsp. low-salt chicken bouillon
    granules
½ tsp. curry powder
1 (10 oz.) can mandarin oranges
1 tsp. lemon juice
1 tsp. cornstarch
1 green pepper, sliced

Trim pork chops; sprinkle with pepper. Coat skillet with cooking spray. Heat on medium until hot. Add pork chops and brown on both sides. Remove and drain on paper towels. Return chops to skillet. Combine water, onion, bouillon, and curry; pour over chops. Bring to a boil, cover, reduce heat, and simmer 45 minutes or until chops are tender. Transfer to a warm platter; keep warm. Drain oranges; reserve syrup. Combine liquid, lemon juice, and cornstarch in small bowl. Add juice mixture and green pepper to skillet. Cook, stirring until thickened. Stir in oranges. Spoon sauce over pork chops.

6 servings. Per serving: 261 calories, 15 g total fat (5 g saturated), 24 g protein,
6 g carbohydrate, 140 mg sodium, 515 mg potassium, 243 mg phosphorus.

Pork Chops and Apples

4-6 pork chops
3-4 unpeeled apples, cored and
    sliced
¼ c. packed brown sugar
½ tsp. cinnamon
2 T. butter

Heat oven to 400 degrees. Brown chops on both sides in hot fat. Place apple slices in greased baking dish. Sprinkle with sugar and cinnamon; dot with butter. Top with chops; cover. Bake for 1½ hours.

6 servings. Per serving: 347 calories, 19 g total fat (8 g saturated), 24 g protein,
20 g carbohydrate, 101 mg sodium, 553 potassium, 243 mg phosphorus.

Pork Chops with White Wine

1 tsp. sage
1 tsp. rosemary, crushed
1 tsp. minced garlic
freshly ground pepper
4 pork loin chops (1″)
2 T. margarine
1 T. olive oil
¾ c. dry white wine, divided
1 T. minced parsley

Trim chops. Combine sage, rosemary, garlic, and pepper. Press mixture into both sides of each chop. In heavy 12-inch skillet, melt margarine with the olive oil over medium heat. When foam subsides, brown chops for 2–3 minutes per side. Remove from pan to a platter. Pour off all but a thin film of fat from pan, add ½ cup of wine and bring to a boil. Return chops to pan, cover and reduce heat to simmer.

Basting with the pan juices occasionally, cook chops for 25 to 30 minutes, or until tender. Transfer chops to heated serving platter. Pour remaining ¼ cup of wine into skillet; boil over high heat, stirring and scraping up brown bits, until reduced to a few tablespoons of syrupy glaze. Remove skillet from heat; stir in parsley. Pour over chops.

4 servings. Per serving: 349 calories, 24 g total fat, (7 g saturated), 24 g protein, 1 g carbohydrate, 62 mg sodium, 467 mg potassium, 240 mg phosphorus.

Quick Skillet Pork Chops

1 T. oil
4 pork loin chops (½″)
¾ c. water
1 T. currant jelly
Low sodium seasoned pepper

In 12-inch skillet over medium-high heat, in hot oil, cook pork chops until browned on both sides, about 10 minutes. Add water; heat to boiling. Reduce heat to low, cover, and simmer 15 minutes or until chops are tender. Remove chops to a warm platter; keep warm. Into liquid in skillet, stir currant jelly; heat through. Pour sauce over chops with seasoned pepper.

> 4 servings. Per serving: 279 calories, 18 g total fat (5 g saturated), 23 g protein, 3 g carbohydrate, 63 mg sodium, 429 potassium, 234 mg phosphorus.

Sweet and Sour Pork

½ c. pineapple juice
2 tsp. vinegar
1 tsp. sherry
½ tsp. low-salt soy sauce
Dash sesame hot oil
Dash fresh-ground pepper
Dash ginger
Dash allspice
2 T. minced green onion
¼ c. sliced green pepper
¼ c. sliced onion
¾ lb. pork, ¼″ strips
2 tsp. chopped parsley
Fresh-ground pepper
1 tsp. cornstarch in 2 T. water

Combine first 7 ingredients in saucepan; heat. Stir in dissolved cornstarch; cook over medium heat, stirring, until thickened; keep warm. Spray nonstick skillet with cooking spray; cook pork till no longer pink. Set aside. Sprinkle green onion, green pepper, and onion in skillet; top with pork, sprinkle with pepper; cook 5 min., add sauce and serve.

4 servings. Per serving: 163 calories, 7 g total fat (2 g saturated), 18 g protein, 6 g carbohydrate, 65 mg sodium, 303 mg potassium, 147 mg phosphorus.

LAMB

BBQ Butterfly Leg of Lamb

1 c. dry red wine
¾ c. beef stock
3 T. orange marmalade
2 T. red wine vinegar
1 T. minced dried onion
1 T. marjoram
1 T. dried rosemary
1 lg. bay leaf, crumbled
¼ tsp. ginger
1 clove crushed garlic
6–7 lb. leg of lamb, boned and
    butterflied

In a 2-quart saucepan combine all ingredients except lamb and simmer uncovered for 20 minutes. Place the butterfly lamb in a 9 x 13 roasting pan. Pour the hot marinade over the lamb and marinate at room temperature 6–8 hours, turning frequently. Barbecue over medium-hot coals for 30 to 45 minutes or until meat thermometer registers 150–160 degrees. Slice fairly thin on a slight diagonal.

16 servings. Per serving: 270 calories, 16 g total fat (7 g saturated), 25 g protein, 4 g carbohydrate, 73 mg sodium, 345 mg potassium, 186 mg phosphorus.

Butterflied Leg of Lamb

1 large leg of lamb
1 lg. bottle low-sodium Italian
   dressing
1 lg. onion, grated
1/2 tsp. thyme
1 1/2 tsp. garlic powder
4 oz. mint jelly
1/2 c. dry white wine

Have butcher bone and butterfly lamb. Combine other ingredients to make a marinade and pour over lamb. Marinate at least 6 hours or overnight. Turn meat occasionally. Barbecue as you would a steak, 15 to 20 minutes. Baste often.

12 servings. Per serving: 293 calories, 16 g total fat (7 g saturated), 22 g protein, 13 g carbohydrate, 225 mg sodium, 306 mg potassium, 169 phosphorus.

Creme de Menthe Lamb Chops

6 loin lamb chops
Pepper
2 T. low-salt soy sauce
1/4 c. creme de menthe

Brown chops in small amount of oil, 4-5 minutes per side. Pour off fat. Add remaining ingredients; stir to blend and spoon over chops.

6 servings. Per serving: 146 calories, 5 g total fat (2 g saturated), 14 g protein, 5 g carbohydrate, 208 mg sodium, 174 mg potassium, 104 mg phosphorus.

Grilled Lamb Chops

2 T. cider vinegar
1–2 cloves crushed garlic
¼ tsp. curry powder
½ tsp. dry mustard
⅛ tsp. cayenne pepper
3 T. oil
6 lamb chops (1½")

With a wire whisk beat together the vinegar, garlic, curry powder, mustard, and cayenne, in a small bowl. Add the oil gradually, beating well. Brush the marinade over both sides of each lamb chop and let the chops stand at room temperature for at least 30 minutes. To barbecue, place th chops about 6 inches from hot coals and grill for about 6–8 minutes per side. To broil in oven, place chops in a broiler pan and broil 4 inches from heat for about 5–6 minutes per side.

6 servings. Per serving: 265 calories, 22 g total fat (7 g saturated), 16 g protein, 1 g carbohydrate, 50 mg sodium, 220 mg potassium, 127 mg phosphorus.

Minted Lamb Chops

1/2 c. dry white wine
1/4 c. water
2 T. oil
1 sm. onion, finely chopped
2 cloves minced garlic
1 T. chopped fresh mint or 1 tsp.
  dried mint
1 tsp. rosemary, crushed
1/4 tsp. pepper
8 shoulder lamb chops

In small bowl combine wine, water, oil, onion, garlic, mint, rosemary, and pepper. Place chops in shallow dish; pour in marinade. Cover; refrigerate overnight, turning occasionally. Drain; reserve marinade. Grill chops 4 to 6 inches over medium-high heat 20 to 25 minutes; turn and brush often with reserved marinade.

8 servings. Per serving: 290 calories, 20 g total fat (7 g saturated), 22 g protein, 2 g carbohydrate, 54 mg sodium, 242 mg potassium, 149 mg phosphorus.

Quick Lamb Curry

2 onions, coarsely chopped
2 T. butter
2 c. cooked lamb, cubed
2 T. flour
Freshly ground pepper
1¼ c. chicken stock
2 tsp. curry powder
2 tart apples, peeled and cut
   in wedges
1 T. raisins

Sauté onions in butter slowly in large, heavy skillet until limp and clear. Add lamb to onion mixture until it is warm. Sprinkle the lamb mixture with the flour. Blend it into meat and onions and add heated chicken stock, stirring constantly until thick. Add curry, apples, raisins, and pepper to taste and simmer, covered for 5–10 minutes, just until apples are cooked. Serve over rice.

4 servings. Per serving: 271 calories, 12 g total fat (6 g saturated), 22 g protein, 21 g carbohydrate, 135 mg sodium, 346 mg potassium, 149 mg phosphorus.

Apple 'n Spice Roast Lamb

4-5 lb. leg of lamb
1/8 tsp. pepper
1 tsp. ground ginger
1/2 tsp. ground nutmeg
1/2 tsp. ground cinnamon
1/4 c. honey
1/4 c. water
1 T. lemon juice
1/4 tsp. ground ginger
1/4 tsp. ground nutmeg
1/4 tsp. ground cinnamon
2 apples, cut in wedges

Rub outside of roast with mixture of pepper, ginger, nutmeg, and cinnamon. Place meat, fat side up, on rack in roasting pan. Insert meat thermometer. Roast, uncovered at 325 degrees for 2 1/2 to 3 1/4 hours for medium doneness (160 degrees.) Transfer to serving platter. Let stand 15 minutes. In medium skillet combine honey, water, lemon juice, and remaining spices; bring to boil. Add apple. Simmer, covered for 8–10 minutes. Serve sauce with meat slices.

10 servings. Per serving: 307 calories, 17 g total fat (7 g saturated), 26 g protein, 12 g carbohydrate, 68 mg sodium, 362 mg potassium, 197 mg phosphorus.

Leg of Lamb with Currant Sauce

6–7 lb. leg of lamb
1½ oz. gin (1 jigger)
2 T. Dijon mustard
1 clove crushed garlic
½ tsp. rosemary
¼ tsp. pepper
2 T. flour
½ c. currant jelly
1¼ c. water
¼ c. gin

Wipe the lamb well and place on a rack in a roasting pan, fat side up. Blend jigger of gin, mustard, garlic, rosemary, and pepper to make a paste. Spread the mixture over the lamb. Roast lamb in a 325 degree over for about 2 hours or until meat thermometer registers 160 degrees. Remove lamb from oven; keep warm.

Remove excess fat from pan drippings. To the drippings add flour, stirring well, and simmer 3 minutes. Add the currant jelly and water and heat, stirring, until the jelly is melted. Add the ¼ cup gin, stirring to blend. Cook, stirring constantly, over medium-low heat until the mixture thickens and boils, about 2–3 minutes. Remove sauce from heat and serve with lamb.

16 servings. Per serving: 289 calories, 16 g total fat (7 g saturated), 25 g protein, 8 g carbohydrate, 114 mg sodium, 311 mg potassium, 118 mg phosphorus.

Leg of Lamb with Herbs

1 c. dry white wine
2 cloves garlic, crushed
1 tsp. ground black pepper
1 tsp. paprika
1 tsp. chopped fresh basil leaves
1 tsp. chopped fresh rosemary
    leaves
1 4 to 5 lb. leg of lamb, boned and
    rolled

In a small bowl, mix together wine and seasonings. Place lamb in shallow glass baking dish. Pour marinade over lamb; cover and refrigerate at least four hour or overnight, turning once.

Preheat oven to 325 degrees. Pour off marinade and reserve. Place lamb on rack in shallow roasting pan. Roast 20 to 25 minutes per pound or until meat thermometer registers 140 to 145 degrees. Bring reserved marinade to a boil and baste lamb occasionally. (Once meat is done, discard any remaining marinade.) Remove from oven and allow to stand for 15 to 20 minutes before slicing.

15 servings. Per serving: 231 calories, 14 g total fat (6 g saturated), 2 g protein,
1 g carbohydrate, 57 mg sodium, 282 mg potassium, 164 mg phosphorus.

Marinated Lamb Shish Kebab

1/4 c. fresh lemon juice
1/2 c. olive oil
1/4 tsp. pepper
1/2 tsp. oregano
1 lg. onion, thinly sliced
3–4 cloves crushed garlic
2 T. minced parsley
2 lb. lamb, cut in 2" cubes
15-20 bay leaves

In heat proof bowl just large enough to hold meat, combine first 4 ingredients and heat. Add onions, garlic, parsley and lamb and mix until meat is coated with marinade. Marinate at room temperature for 6 hours or refrigerate overnight. Skewer lamb, alternating with bay leaves, dividing meat equally. Broil 3 inches from heat for about 10 minutes, or until pink inside, turning occasionally to brown evenly. Discard bay leaves. Serve lamb with rice pilaf.

10 servings. Per serving: 264 calories, 17 g total fat (4 g saturated), 23 g protein, 4 g carbohydrate, 50 mg sodium, 218 mg potassium, 147 mg phosphorus.

Shish Kebab with Red Wine Marinade

2 lb. boneless lamb
1 c. dry red wine
1 clove minced garlic
$\frac{1}{2}$ tsp. fresh-ground pepper
$\frac{1}{2}$ tsp. thyme
$\frac{1}{2}$ c. minced parsley
2 green peppers, cut in $\frac{1}{2}$"
   squares
12 small white onions, cut in half

Cut the lamb into $\frac{1}{2}$-inch cubes. In a bowl combine the wine, garlic, pepper, thyme, oregano, and parsley. Marinate the lamb in the mixture for 12 hours, basting and turning occasionally. When ready to cook, drain lamb, reserving marinade. Use 8 skewers to thread lamb, green pepper, and onions, starting and ending with lamb. Broil in broiler or over charcoal to desired degree of doneness. Turn frequently and baste with the marinade.

8 servings. Per serving: 258 calories, 8 g total fat (3 g saturated), 30 g protein,
11 g carbohydrate, 67 mg sodium, 476 mg potassium, 219 mg phosphorus.

Plum-Scrumptious Lamb Kebabs

1 can (17 oz.) purple plums,
    drained, reserve syrup
3 T. lemon juice
1 T. low-salt soy sauce
1 tsp. Worcestershire sauce
1 clove crushed garlic
½ tsp. basil
2 lb. lamb cubes
Freshly ground pepper

Pit plums and sieve. Add ¼ cup reserved syrup and next 5 ingredients, mix well. Add meat and marinate overnight. Skewer meat and sprinkle with pepper. Grill over coals, basting and turning until done. Heat remainder of marinade and serve with meat.

8 servings. Per serving: 220 calories, 8 g total fat (3 g saturated), 29 g protein, 10 g carbohydrate, 130 mg sodium, 331 mg potassium, 185 mg phosphorus.

Chapter **6**

POULTRY

Apricot-Glazed Chicken

1 lg. chicken breast, boned
    and halved
1 T. butter
$\frac{1}{3}$ c. apricot preserves
1$\frac{1}{2}$ T. lemon juice
1 tsp. low-sodium lemon-pepper

Arrange chicken in shallow pan dotted with the butter. In a saucepan combine the apricot preserves, lemon juice, and lemon pepper. Blend well. Heat until preserves melt. Pour sauce over chicken and bake, uncovered, at 350 degrees for 40 to 45 minutes, basting occasionally. Recipe is easily doubled.

2 servings. Per serving: 332 calories, 12 g total fat (5 g saturated), 22 g protein, 36 g carbohydrate, 235 mg sodium, 265 mg potassium, 160 mg phosphorus.

BBQ Chicken

2 (1¼ lb.) broilers, quartered
2 T. oil
½ c. water
⅓ c. cider vinegar
1 tsp. Worcestershire sauce
½ tsp. freshly ground pepper
1 tsp. chili powder
3 T. catsup
2 tsp. sugar
½ tsp. dry mustard

Heat 1 T. oil in a baking pan and place the broilers in it, skin side down. Broil in a hot broiler 15 minutes. Combine and bring to a boil the water, vinegar, Worcestershire, pepper, chili powder, catsup, sugar, mustard and remaining 1 T. oil. At the end of 15 minutes, turn chicken over, pour sauce over them and broil 20 minutes longer or until tender. Baste frequently.

8 servings. Per serving: 245 calories, 12 g total fat (3 g saturated), 31 g protein,
4 g carbohydrate, 84 mg sodium, 300 mg potassium, 233 mg phosphorus.

BBQ Drunken Chicken

¼ c. lemon juice
2 T. + 2 tsp. margarine, melted
6 oz. (¾ c.) light beer
3 minced garlic cloves
1 tsp. low-sodium lemon-pepper
8 bone-in chicken breast halves, skinned

In a 3 qt. baking dish, combine first 5 ingredients; add chicken pieces and turn to coat. Cover, refrigerate overnight, turning chicken occasionally. Spray grill rack with nonstick cooking spray; place 5" from coals. Place chicken bone-side down on rack and grill 20 minutes, brushing with marinade. Turn chicken, brush with marinade and cook 10–15 minutes, until cooked through.

8 servings. Per serving: 237 calories, 12 g total fat (3 g saturated), 29 g protein, 1 g carbohydrate, 95 mg sodium, 260 mg potassium, 215 mg phosphorus.

Chicken Fricassee

3½ lb. fryer, cut up
¼ c. flour
½ tsp. pepper
2 T. oil
1 c. chopped onion
1 clove minced garlic
¾ c. boiling water

Roll chicken in mixture of flour and pepper. Heat oil in Dutch oven or heavy saucepan; brown chicken and onions in it. Stir in garlic. Add the water; cover and cook over low heat 45 minutes or until tender. Add extra water if necessary.

10 servings. Per serving: 267 calories, 12 g total fat (3 g saturated), 35 g protein, 4 g carbohydrate, 82 mg sodium, 311 mg potassium, 254 mg phosphorus.

Chicken Hawaiian

1 fryer, cut in eights
¹/₄ c. flour
¹/₂ c. shortening
1 c. sugar
1 c. pineapple juice
1 T. lemon juice
2 c. fresh cranberries

Combine flour and pepper in a bag and shake chicken to coat. Brown chicken lightly on all sides in shortening; drain. One hour before serving, arrange chicken in single layer in shallow baking pan. Combine sugar, pineapple juice, and lemon juice in saucepan. Bring to boil, stirring to dissolve sugar. Boil 5 minutes. Add cranberries and cook without stirring for 5 minutes until berries pop. Pour over chicken, basting occasionally with sauce while baking at 350 degrees for 40 minutes. Serve chicken with sauce.

8 servings. Per serving: 454 calories, 21 g total fat (5 g saturated), 31 g protein, 35 g carbohydrate, 73 mg sodium, 316 mg potassium, 228 mg phosphorus.

Chicken Imperial

2 c. dry bread crumbs
¼ c. minced parsley
1 clove minced garlic
⅛ tsp. pepper
1 c. sweet butter, melted
1 T. Dijon mustard
1 tsp. Worcestershire sauce
8 chicken breasts

Skin, bone and halve chicken breasts. In a medium bowl combine the bread crumbs, parsley, garlic, and pepper. Mix together the melted butter, mustard, and Worcestershire. Dip the chicken first into butter mixture and then roll in the crumb mixture, coating all sides. Place the pieces in a foil-lined shallow baking pan, just large enough to hold the pieces in 1 layer. Sprinkle the chicken with the remaining butter mixture and bake uncovered at 350 degrees for about 1 hour or until tender.

16 servings. Per serving: 249 calories, 16 g total fat (8 g saturated), 16 g protein, 9 g carbohydrate, 288 mg sodium, 161 mg potassium, 129 mg phosphorus.

Chicken Marsala

1 2½–3 lb. fryer, cut up
Freshly ground pepper
¼ tsp. garlic powder
¼ tsp. paprika
⅛ tsp. thyme
¼ c. Parmesan cheese
1 T. minced parsley
⅓ c. fine bread crumbs
⅓ c. water
1 T. oil
¼ c. margarine, melted
⅓ c. marsala wine

In a paper bag place seasonings, cheese, parsley, and crumbs; coat chicken by shaking a few pieces at a time in the bag. Oil a shallow roasting pan, pour in the water and arrange chicken pieces. Sprinkle chicken with oil and margarine and bake at 350 degrees, uncovered, for 30 minutes. Pour wine over chicken. Lower oven heat to 325 degrees; cover pan with foil and bake 15 minutes longer. Remove foil; raise oven heat to 350 degrees, and bake 10 minutes longer.

8 servings. Per serving: 313 calories, 17 g total fat (4 g saturated), 35 g protein, 4 g carbohydrate, 110 mg sodium, 305 mg potassium, 227 mg phosphorus.

Chicken Oriental

1 3 lb. fryer, cut up
1/3 c. flour
1/8 tsp. pepper
1/4 c. butter
1 c. canned pineapple chunks
1 T. cornstarch
1/2 c. pineapple juice
2 T. low-sodium soy sauce

Coat chicken with flour and pepper. Fry chicken in butter. Mix cornstarch, pineapple juice and soy sauce. Add pineapple chunks. Pour over chicken. Serve with rice.

12 servings. Per serving: 226 calories, 10 g total fat (4 g saturated), 25 g protein, 7 g carbohydrate, 181 mg sodium, 231 mg potassium, 181 mg phosphorus.

Chicken Paprikash

3 1/2 lb. fryer, cut up
1/4 tsp. pepper
3 T. oil
1 c. chopped onion
1 T. paprika
3/4 c. boiling water
3 T. nonfat dry milk powder
1/4 c. water

Rub chicken with pepper. Heat oil in a deep skillet; brown the chicken in it and remove. In remaining oil, sauté the onions until browned. Stir in paprika, then the water. Return the chicken; cover and cook over low heat 45 minutes. Mix the dry milk and water; stir into the gravy; heat.

12 servings. Per serving: 232 calories, 1 g total fat (3 g saturated), 29 g protein, 3 g carbohydrate, 79 mg sodium, 302 mg potassium, 228 mg phosphorus.

Chicken Piccata

lb. (4 pieces) boneless, skinless
    chicken breasts, pounded
    1/4 inch thick
1/4 tsp. black pepper
2 T. flour
1 T. vegetable oil
3/4 c. reduced-sodium chicken
    broth
3/4 tsp. dried rosemary leaves,
    crushed
1 T. lemon juice
1 T. butter

Season chicken with pepper. Dredge in flour. Sauté half the chicken in half the oil in skillet over medium high heat until golden, 4 to 6 minutes. Remove to platter; keep warm. Repeat with remaining oil and chicken.

Add broth and rosemary to skillet. Boil to reduce by half. Stir in lemon juice and butter until butter melts. Return chicken to skillet; heat through.

4 servings. Per serving: 198 calories, 9 g total fat (3 g saturated), 24 g protein, 4 g carbohydrate, 105 mg sodium, 202 mg potassium, 174 mg phosphorus.

Chicken and Pineapple

1 3–4 lb. chicken, cut up
½ tsp. pepper
2 T. butter
1 lg. can sliced pineapple
2 T. oil
1 lg. onion
1 (10 oz.) pkg. frozen peas
Chicken stock

Sprinkle pepper on chicken pieces. Drain pineapple, reserving juice. Arrange chicken pieces closely together in shallow baking pan. Broil about 3 inches from heat until chicken begins to brown. Turn to brown evenly.

Melt butter in heavy skillet and lightly brown the pineapple. Remove from skillet. Add the oil and cook onion rings until golden. Add onion to browned chicken. Measure the pineapple juice and add enough chicken stock to make 2 cups. Pour over chicken. Bake at 350 degrees for 30 minutes. Add pineapple slices and defrosted peas. Continue baking for about 20 minutes or until done.

12 servings. Per serving: 253 calories, 11 g total fat (3 g saturated), 26 g protein, 12 g carbohydrate, 115 mg sodium, 251 mg potassium, 163 mg phosphorus.

Honey Barbecued Chicken

1 2½–3 lb. fryer, cut up
1 egg yolk
⅛ tsp. pepper
½ tsp. paprika
2 T. low-salt soy sauce
2 T. lemon juice
¼ c. honey
2 T. butter, melted

Beat egg yolk slightly in bowl; blend in remaining ingredients. Dip chicken pieces into sauce and place in a 9 x 12 x 2-inch baking pan. Pour remaining sauce over chicken. Bake uncovered for 30 minutes at 400 degrees. Turn chicken, baste with sauce in pan. Continue baking for 35-40 minutes until chicken is tender.

8 servings. Per serving: 271 calories, 12 g total fat (4 g saturated), 31 g protein, 10 g carbohydrate, 229 mg sodium, 267 mg potassium, 231 mg phosphorus.

Honey Mustard Chicken

¼ c. lemon juice
2 T. Dijon mustard
2 T. honey
1 tsp. ginger
1 tsp. rosemary
2 lb. skinless chicken thighs
½ c. dried bread crumbs

Combine the lemon juice, mustard, honey, ginger, and rosemary in a small bowl. Place the chicken between sheets of waxed paper and pound to equal thickness. Pour half the honey-mustard mixture over chicken; cover and refrigerated for 20 minutes.

Set oven to broil. Sprinkle the bread crumbs over top of chicken and broil for 7 to 8 minutes. In a saucepan, warm remaining sauce and serve with the chicken.

8 servings. Per serving: 286 calories, 13 g total fat (4 g saturated), 31 g protein, 10 g carbohydrate, 249 mg sodium, 308 mg potassium, 226 mg phosphorus.

Lemon Chicken

3 lemons
3 lb. chicken
1 tsp. rosemary
1 tsp. oregano
½ tsp. pepper
½ bunch fresh parsley,
    or ¼ c. dried
3 cloves minced garlic
1 T. olive oil
½ tsp. sugar
2–3 carrots, sliced thin
1 onion, cut in eights
½ c. water

Preheat oven to 450 degrees. Lay a long sheet of foil over a roasting pan. Slice on of the lemons and layer slices on the foil. Loosen skin from chicken and remove all visible fat. Using a knife, carefully remove all skin from breast, leaving skin on drumsticks and wings. Place the chicken on top of the lemon slices in the roasting pan.

In a small bowl, combine to form a paste: rosemary, oregano, pepper, parsley, garlic, oil, sugar, and the juice of the 2 remaining lemons. Rub some of the paste in the cavity of the chicken; truss the chicken. Use the rest of the paste to coat the bird. Scatter carrot slices over and around the chicken; scatter onion around chicken. Bring up foil and seal around chicken. Pour water in bottom of the pan. Turn oven down to 400 degrees. Put chicken in oven. Bake 1 hour.

10 servings. Per serving: 260 calories, 18 g total fat (5 g saturated), 19 g protein, 6 g carbohydrate, 91 mg sodium, 324 mg potassium, 173 mg phosphorus.

Lemon Chicken Breasts

1 lb. boneless chicken breast
halves
1/4 c. flour
1/4 tsp. dried oregano, crushed
1/4 tsp. ground black pepper
2 T. butter
1/4 c. low sodium chicken broth
2 T. lemon juice

Dip chicken in flour combined with pepper and oregano. In 12-inch skillet, melt butter over medium-high heat and cook chicken until lightly browned, turning once. Add broth and lemon juice and simmer 8 minutes or until chicken is done.

4 servings. Per serving: 244 calories, 12 g total fat (5 g saturated), 25 g protein, 7 g carbohydrate, 124 mg sodium, 223 mg potassium, 186 mg phosphorus.

Mandarin Chicken

1 fryer, cut up
1/4 c. flour
2 T. margarine
2 T. oil
4 T. lemon juice
1/2 c. pineapple juice
2 T. honey
1/2 T. low-salt soy sauce
1/2 tsp. powdered ginger
1 (11 oz.) can mandarin oranges

Shake chicken in paper bag with flour to coat. In a skillet, heat oil and margarine; add chicken and brown. Drain mandarin oranges and set aside. Mix juice from can with lemon juice, pineapple juice, honey, soy sauce, and ginger. Pour sauce over chicken in skillet. Cover and simmer for 30 minutes. Add orange sections 5 minutes before serving.

8 servings. Per serving: 321 calories, 14 g total fat (3 g saturated), 31 g protein, 14 g carbohydrate, 107 mg sodium, 342 mg potassium, 229 mg phosphorus.

Orange Marmalade-Curry Chicken

4 floured breasts, thighs, or
    drumsticks
Butter or margarine
1/2 c. orange marmalade
1/2 c. warm water
1/2 tsp. (or more) curry
Pepper to taste

Brown chicken in butter. Mix together marmalade, water, and curry powder. Baste chicken with this mixture. Pour remaining mixture into frying pan; cover and cook for 30 minutes or until chicken is tender. Remove cover during last 5 minutes of cooking.

6 servings. Per serving: 212 calories. 7 g total fat (3 g saturated), 20 g protein, 18 g carbohydrate, 82 mg sodium, 174 mg potassium, 143 mg phosphorus.

Oven Fried Lemon Chicken

1/2 c. lemon juice
1 T. low-salt soy sauce
1/2 tsp. pepper
1/4 c. oil
2 T. grated lemon peel
1 clove crushed garlic
2 1/2–3 lb. fryer, cut up
1/2 c. flour
1/4 tsp. paprika
1/2 c. butter or margarine

Mix lemon juice, soy sauce, pepper, oil, lemon peel, and garlic together; let stand for several hours. Shake chicken pieces in bag with flour and paprika. Melt butter in pan; add chicken pieces. Pour lemon sauce over chicken. Bake at 350 degrees for 1 hour or until tender.

12 servings. Per serving: 226 calories, 17 g total fat (7 g saturated), 21 g protein, 5 g carbohydrate, 167 mg sodium, 192 mg potassium, 155 mg phosphorus.

Pineapple Chicken

2 whole chicken breasts
1/4 tsp. pepper
3 T. cornstarch
1 (1 lb.) can pineapple chunks
3 T. oil
2 T. low-salt soy sauce
2 tsp. lemon juice

Remove skin and bones of chicken; cut meat in 2-inch pieces. Mix together pepper and 2 T. cornstarch; toss with chicken pieces. Drain pineapple, reserving 3/4 c. juice. Heat oil in skillet; sauté the chicken 10 minutes. Add the pineapple; cover and cook over low heat 5 minutes. Mix the remaining cornstarch with the soy sauce, lemon juice, and pineapple juice. Add to the skillet, stirring to the boiling point. Cook 3 minutes; don't overcook.

4 servings. Per serving: 286 calories, 14 g total fat (2 g saturated), 16 g protein, 25 g carbohydrate, 289 mg sodium, 263 mg potassium, 113 mg phosphorus.

Roast Chicken in a Bag

1/4 tsp. pepper
1/2 tsp. paprika
1 clove minced garlic
1/4 c. olive oil
1 (5–6 lb.) roasting chicken
Large heavy brown paper bag

Combine all seasonings with oil and rub chicken with mixture. Place in bag and close tightly. Place in roasting pan; bake at 325 degrees for 2 1/2 hours. Bag may be removed for last half hour to brown chicken.

8 servings. Per serving: 261 calories, 15 g total fat (3 g saturated), 30 g protein, 0 g carbohydrate, 90 mg sodium 280 mg potassium, 231 mg phosphorus.

Sesame BBQ Chicken

2½–3 lb. fryer, cut up
⅛ c. low-salt soy sauce
⅛ c. sherry
2 T. sugar
1 tsp. ground ginger
1 tsp. sesame hot oil
2 T. sesame seeds, toasted
2 T. oil

Marinate chicken for 1–2 hours in soy sauce, sherry, sugar, ginger, and sesame hot oil. Remove from marinade and broil over charcoal or in oven, basting with marinade and oil. When chicken is done and browned on both sides (about 30 minutes), sprinkle with toasted sesame seeds and serve.

8 servings. Per serving: 271 calories, 13 g total fat (3 g saturated), 31 g protein, 4 g carbohydrate, 203 mg sodium, 256 mg potassium, 219 mg phosphorus.

Sesame Chicken

2 T. butter
2 T. oil
2½–3 lb. fryer, cut up
⅓ c. flour seasoned with pepper
3 T. sesame seeds
2–3 T. minced green onion
½ c. white wine
Juice of ½ lemon

Melt butter with oil in baking pan. Allow to cool slightly. In a bag, shake chicken with seasoned flour until coated. Roll pieces in oil in baking pan; arrange so that pieces do not touch. Sprinkle with lemon juice and sesame seeds. Bake at 375 degrees for 30 minutes, or until lightly browned. Turn chicken; sprinkle with sesame seeds and minced onion. Pour wine in pan and cook 30-45 minutes, basting frequently.

8 servings. Per serving: 306 calories, 16 g total fat (4 g saturated), 32 g protein, 5 g carbohydrate, 209 mg sodium, 280 mg potassium, 228 mg phosphorus.

Burgundy-Braised Cornish Hen

1 Cornish hen
1/3 c. Burgundy wine
1/3 c. red-wine vinegar
1/2 tsp. rosemary, crushed
1/8 tsp. thyme
2 large cloves garlic, minced

Remove giblets from hen, and discard; rinse with cold water. Remove skin; split hen lengthwise. Place hen, meaty side down, in a square baking dish. Combine remaining ingredients, stirring well; pour over hen. Bake at 325 degrees for 20 minutes; turn hen over, and bake an additional hour, basting every 15 minutes. Broil 6 inches from heat 5 minutes.

> 2 servings. Per serving: 229 calories, 10 g total fat (3 g saturated), 21 g protein, 7 g carbohydrate, 242 mg sodium, 294 mg potassium, 149 mg phosphorus.

Apple Glazed Turkey Breast

1/3 c. honey
1 T. dry mustard
6–7 lb. fresh turkey breast
1 (6 oz.) can frozen apple juice
   concentrated, thawed

Skin turkey breast. Combine honey, mustard, and apple juice concentrate. Place turkey breast on a rack in a roasting pan; insert meat thermometer into meaty portion so that it does not touch bone. Baste with honey mixture. Cover and bake at 325 degrees for 1 hour. Uncover and bake an additional hour, or until meat thermometer registers 170 degrees, basting frequently with honey mixture. Let cool 10 to 15 minutes before slicing.

> 22 servings. Per serving: 190 calories, 7 g total fat (2 g saturated), 24 g protein, 7 g carbohydrate, 50 mg sodium, 277 mg potassium, 177 mg phosphorus.

Glazed Turkey Breast

3 T. butter
1 fresh or frozen boneless turkey
   breast half (3 lb.), thawed if
   frozen
1/4 c. apple jelly
1 tsp. dried thyme
Freshly ground pepper to taste

In small microwave bowl, cook butter on high until melted, 30 to 45 seconds. Set aside. Place turkey breast, skin side down, on microwave rack in 12 x 8-inch microwave baking dish; brush with half of melted butter. Cook, covered with wax paper, on medium (50% power) 2 minutes. Turn breast skin side up; brush with butter. Cook on medium (50% power) 15 to 25 minutes longer until instant read thermometer inserted in thickest part of breast registers 160 degrees F. Remove from oven.

In small microwave bowl, cook apple jelly on high (100% power) 30 to 45 seconds until melted; brush over turkey. Sprinkle with pepper and thyme. Return to microwave and cook 1 minute on high until turkey is well glazed.

Let turkey breast stand, covered loosely with foil, until meat thermometer registers 170 degrees. Slice and serve accompanied by apricot chutney mustard if desired.

> 12 servings. Per serving: 179 calories, 4 g total fat (4 g saturated), 30 g protein,
> 5 g carbohydrate, 84 mg sodium, 296 mg potassium, 222 mg phosphorus.

Apricot Chutney Mustard: In small bowl, stir 1/2 c. apricot preserves, 1/4 c. mango chutney, and 1 T. country style Dijon mustard to blend well. Makes 3/4 c.

Grilled Lemon Turkey Breast

¼ c. lemon juice
2 T. olive oil
1 tsp. minced garlic
1 tsp. Dijon mustard
1 tsp. dried leaf sage
½ tsp. dried leaf marjoram
¼ tsp. pepper
1 2 lb. boneless turkey breast half

Combine lemon juice, olive oil, garlic, mustard, sage, marjoram, and pepper in a gallon-size plastic food storage bag. Add turkey; refrigerate 24 hours, turning bag occasionally.

Fold piece of heavy-duty aluminum foil in half, dull side out, to form 18-inch square. Place turkey in middle of square, drizzle marinade over. Fold foil over and seal tightly all around.

Prepare grill so coals are medium-hot. Push coals to two sides of grill; add a few more briquettes to each side. Grill packet 5 to 6 inches over medium-hot coals in covered grill for 25 minutes; turn over after 15 minutes. Remove packet from grill; remove turkey from packet, reserving juices in packet for basting. Place turkey directly on grid. Grill, basting with reserved juices and turning over, 20 to 30 minutes longer or until cooked through (170 degrees in thickest part of breast). Remove from grill; let stand 5 minutes. Slice.

8 servings. Per serving: 167 calories, 4 g total fat (1 g saturated), 30 g protein,
1 g carbohydrate, 67 mg sodium, 302 mg potassium, 224 mg phosphorus.

Herbed Turkey Cutlets

2 medium lemons
3/4 tsp. dried sage
1 T. vegetable oil
1/4 tsp. coarsely ground black
    pepper
1 garlic clove, crushed
1 lb. turkey cutlets

From lemons, grate enough peel to make 2 tsp. Cut each lemon in half; squeeze juice from 3 halves into small bowl. Into lemon juice stir lemon peel, sage, oil, pepper, and garlic. Place turkey cutlets on grill over high heat. Cook 5 to 7 minutes, brushing with lemon mixture often and turning once until turkey just loses its pink color throughout. Arrange cutlets on serving platter; squeeze remaining lemon half over cutlets.

4 servings. Per serving: 174 calories, 4 g total fat, (0 g saturated), 30 g protein, 3 g carbohydrate, 52 mg sodium, 333 mg potassium, 227 mg phosphorus.

Overnight Turkey

1 20 lb. turkey
1/2 stick butter
1 lg. clove garlic, slivered
1 lg. onion, quartered
1 lg. unpeeled apple, quartered

Rinse turkey and wipe dry. Rub inside and out with half the butter. Place remaining butter inside turkey. Place garlic, onion and apple in cavity. Do not season inside turkey. Place breast-side down on rack in roaster. Bake for 1 hour at 325 degrees. Turn bird on back and reduce heat to 200 degrees. Bake, uncovered, without opening oven, for 10 to 12 hours.

40 servings. Per serving: 206 calories, 7 g total fat (3 g saturated), 33 g protein, 1 g carbohydrate, 91 mg sodium, 348 mg potassium, 242 mg phosphorus.

Turkey Loaf

½ c. low-sodium chicken broth
⅓ c. fresh bread crumbs
2 lb. ground turkey
1 large egg white, lightly beaten
½ c. shredded carrots
1 small onion, grated
½ tsp. dried thyme
½ c. chopped fresh parsley
1 tsp. minced garlic
½ tsp. freshly ground pepper

Preheat oven to 350 degrees F. Pour chicken broth over bread crumbs in small bowl; let stand 10 minutes. Gently mix remaining ingredients in a large bowl. Add bread crumb mixture and mix well. Spoon into a 11/2 quart loaf pan. Bake one hour or until juices run clear.

8 servings. Per serving: 207 calories, 11 g total fat (3 g saturated), 23 g protein, 3 g carbohydrate, 121 mg sodium, 285 mg potassium, 170 mg phosphorus.

Turkey Medallions

3 lb. ground turkey
2¼ c. fresh bread crumbs
1¾ tsp. fennel, crushed
1½ tsp. sage
¼ tsp. allspice
2 egg whites
Flour
3 T. oil
½ c. water
2 T. dry white wine
1 T. butter

In large bowl, mix turkey, bread crumbs, fennel, sage, allspice and egg. With well floured hands, shape turkey mixture into 1-inch balls. With palms of hands, flatten balls into 1/4-inch thick patties.

In 12-inch skillet over medium-high heat, in hot oil, cook patties, a few at a time, until turkey loses its pink color and is browned on both sides, removing patties to large plate as they brown and adding more oil if necessary; keep warm.

Into drippings remaining in skillet over medium-high heat, stir water, wine, and butter, stirring to loosen brown bits from bottom of skillet. To serve, spoon turkey medallions into large chafing dish. Pour pan drippings over turkey patties.

12 servings. Per serving: 266 calories, 16 g total fat (4 g saturated), 24 g protein, 7 g carbohydrate, 148 mg sodium, 245 mg potassium, 172 mg phosphorus.

Turkey Patties

2 lg. egg whites
1/2 slice firm white bread, torn in
    small pieces
1 lb. ground turkey
3 c. finely shredded cabbage
1/3 c. grated onion
1 1/2 tsp. ground coriander
3/4-1 tsp. fresh ground pepper
1/4 tsp. nutmeg
1/4 tsp. sugar
2 T. butter or margarine

Beat egg in large bowl; stir in bread. Soak a few minutes, then whisk to break up bread. Add remaining ingredients, except butter, and mix until blended. Shape into patties. Melt 1 T. butter in a large skillet over medium heat. Add half of patties; cook turning once, until browned, about 12 minutes. Remove to serving platter and keep warm. Repeat with remaining butter and patties.

5 servings. Per serving: 225 calories, 14 g total fat (5 g saturated), 20 g protein, 6 g carbohydrate, 162 mg sodium, 332 mg potassium, 148 mg phosphorus.

Turkey Slices with Paprika Sauce

1 lb. turkey breast slices
2 egg whites
1 c. bread crumbs
1/4 tsp. pepper
3 T. minced onion
Butter or margarine
1/8 tsp. garlic powder
2 T. flour
1 T. paprika
1 1/2 c. chicken stock
1/4 c. white wine
2 T. sour cream

Make 2 to 4 cuts through membrane on outer edges of turkey slices. Slightly pound out each slice between 2 sheets of waxed paper. Beat egg in shallow bowl; combine bread crumbs and pepper. Dip breast slices in egg, then in bread crumbs. In a medium saucepan, saute onion in 1 T. butter until soft. Stir in garlic powder, flour and paprika. Cook 1 to 2 minutes. Gradually stir in chicken stock and wine. Cook over low heat, stirring often, until sauce comes to a boil and is slightly thickened. Meanwhile, melt 3 T. butter in a large skillet. Sauté breaded turkey slices in butter until golden brown, turning once. Remove turkey slices to heated platter as they brown, adding more butter as needed. To serve, stir sour cream into paprika sauce and serve with turkey breast slices.

6 servings. Per serving: 288 calories, 15 g total fat (7 g saturated), 21 g protein, 17 g carbohydrate, 303 mg sodium, 289 mg potassium, 162 mg phosphorus.

Duckling 'a L'Orange

2 ducklings
2 bay leaves
Lemon juice

Sauce

$\frac{1}{2}$ c. honey
1 c. chicken stock
$\frac{1}{4}$ c. port wine
$\frac{1}{4}$ c. red wine vinegar
2 crushed garlic cloves
$\frac{1}{2}$ tsp. tarragon
$\frac{1}{8}$ tsp. rosemary
1 c. orange marmalade
Orange slices for garnish

Wipe the ducklings with a damp cloth. Sprinkle with lemon juice. Tuck bay leaves in cavity. Roast in 350 degrees oven until golden, pour off fat, cool, and quarter. Discard bay leaves and return to roasting pans, cut side down. While ducklings are roasting, combine sauce ingredients in a saucepan and blend well over medium heat. Pour over quartered ducks, cover and bake at 300 degrees for 1 hour. Uncover and baste. Continue baking for 15 minutes. Garnish with orange slices.

4 servings. Per serving: 520 calories, 14 g total fat (5 g saturated), 10 g protein, 94 g carbohydrates, 103 mg sodium, 216 mg potassium, 83 mg phosphorus.

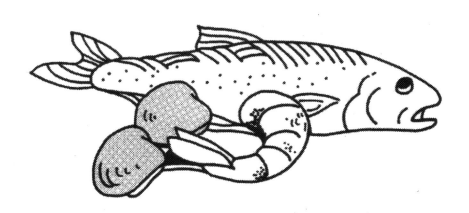

Chapter 7

SEAFOOD

Baked Crumbed Fish

2 lb. swordfish or other fish
Ground pepper
Mayonnaise
1 T. minced onion
$\frac{1}{3}$ c. low-salt Ritz® cracker
    crumbs

Sprinkle fish with pepper. Spread generous layer of mayonnaise on fish, sprinkle with minced onion and top with cracker crumbs. Bake at 400 degrees for 30 minutes.

8 servings. Per serving: 242 calories, 16 g total fat (3 g saturated), 23 g protein, 1 g carbohydrate, 167 mg sodium, 341 mg potassium, 304 mg phosphorus.

Batter-Baked Fish Fillets

1 lb. flounder
6 T. flour
¼ tsp. baking powder
2 egg whites
Paprika & pepper

Thaw fish, if frozen, and rinse in milk. Pat dry. Fork whip egg and oil together in a shallow bowl. Dip the fish pieces first in the flour, then in egg-oil mixture, then once more in flour. Arrange fish fillets on a nonstick cookie sheet. Place in 450 degree oven for 6 minutes. Turn, sprinkle generously with paprika and pepper. Bake 3–4 minutes more.

4 servings. Per serving: 143 calories, 1 g total fat (0 g saturated), 22 g protein, 9 g carbohydrate, 140 mg sodium, 308 mg potassium, 248 mg phosphorus.

Braised Fish Fillets

¼ c. oil
1 lb. firm-textured fish
2 T. flour
½ tsp. sugar
1 tsp. ginger
¼ tsp. garlic powder
½ T. low-salt soy sauce
2 T. sherry
Water
Freshly ground pepper
Chives
1 T. chopped parsley

Dust fillets lightly with flour. In a heavy skillet, heat oil and brown fish on both sides. Combine sugar, ginger, and garlic with soy sauce, sherry, and enough water to make 1 cup. Pour over fish, cover and braise 10 minutes. Uncover, add pepper, chives, and parsley. Cook uncovered 5 minutes more.

4 servings. Per serving: 245 calories, 17 g total fat (2 g saturated), 16 g protein, 5 g carbohydrate, 134 mg sodium, 247 mg potassium, 210 mg phosphorus.

Brazilian Broiled Fish

2 lb. halibut steaks
2 T. lemon juice
1 T. instant coffee
1/4 c. melted margarine or oil
1 tsp. onion powder
Chopped parsley

Place fish steaks in shallow baking dish. Dissolve coffee in lemon juice, add remaining ingredients, except parsley, and mix well. Pour over fish and let stand 30 minutes, turning once. Remove fish, reserving sauce, and broil 4–5 minutes about 3-inches from heat. Turn and brush with sauce. Broil 4–5 minutes more. Sprinkle with parsley.

8 servings. Per serving: 166 calories, 8 g total fat (1 g saturated), 22 g protein, 1 g carbohydrate, 57 mg sodium, 497 mg potassium, 232 mg phosphorus.

Crispy Fish Sticks

3 (1 oz.) slices French bread, cubed
3 T. mayonnaise
2 tsp. water
1 tsp. lemon juice
1/2 tsp. grated lemon rind
1 1/2 lb. whitefish fillets, cut into
    1-inch wide strips

Position knife blade in food processor bowl; add bread cubes. Process 30 seconds or until crumbs are fine. Sprinkle crumbs on an ungreased baking sheet and bake at 350 degrees for 15 minutes or until browned. Place in a shallow bowl and set aside.

Combine mayonnaise, water, juice, and rind in shallow bowl; stir well. Dip fish in mayonnaise mixture, and dredge in bread crumbs. Place fish on a baking sheet coated with cooking spray. Bat at 425 degrees for 25 minutes or until outside is crispy and browned.

8 servings. Per serving: 197 calories, 10 g total fat (2 g saturated), 18 g protein, 7 g carbohydrate, 154 mg sodium, 294 mg potassium, 250 mg phosphorus.

Fish En Papillote

1 lb. sole fillets
½ tsp. pepper
3 T. oil
2 T. grated onion
T. minced parsley
4 T. dry white wine

Season the fish with pepper. Cut pieces of foil large enough to wrap the fillets. Brush one side of the foil with a little oil. Place a fillet in the center of each piece; sprinkle with the onions, parsley, wine, and remaining oil. Bring the foil up over the top of the fish and double fold the edges to form a tight package. Bring the ends up and fold over. Arrange the packages on a baking sheet. Bake in a 425 degree oven 25 minutes. Serve in foil packet.

4 servings. Per serving: 206 calories, 11 g total fat (1 g saturated), 21 g protein, 1 g carbohydrate, 94 mg sodium, 438 mg potassium, 212 mg phosphorus.

Fish Matelote with Red Wine

2 lb. fish (perch, pike or haddock)
1 carrot, sliced
1 onion, minced
2 cloves garlic, halved
$1/4$ tsp. pepper
2 c. red wine
3 T. brandy
3 T. butter, melted
2 T. flour

Clean, wash and dry fish; place in skillet. Add carrot, onion, garlic, pepper, and wine; bring to a boil. Heat 3 T. brandy in a small saucepan; ignite and immediately pour over fish. When flame has burned off, cover the pan; cook fish slowly 15-20 minutes. Remove fish to a warm serving platter; keep hot. Strain and reserve cooking liquid. In the same skillet blend butter and flour. Cook over low heat until mixture bubbles. Remove from heat; gradually stir in reserved cooking liquid. Cook rapidly stirring until sauce thickens. Boil 1-2 minutes longer; pour sauce over fish. Serve with croutons browned with garlic butter.

8 servings. Per serving: 219 calories, 5 g total fat (3 g saturated), 24 g protein, 5 g carbohydrate, 127 mg sodium, 454 mg potassium, 232 mg phosphorus.

Grilled Fish Steaks

1 1/2 lb. fish steaks
3 cloves garlic
1/2tsp. ginger
Juice of 3 lemons
1 tsp. thyme
2 T. olive oil
2 tsp. dry mustard
1/4 tsp. pepper

Place fish in a glass baking dish. To make marinade, combine all other ingredients in a blender or food processor, blending until smooth. Pour marinade over fish; cover and refrigerate at least 1 hour. Cook on outside grill until firm and opaque white. Do not overcook.

6 servings. Per serving: 146 calories, 8 g total fat (1 g saturated), 16 g protein, 4 g carbohydrate, 70 mg sodium, 272 mg potassium, 209 mg phosphorus.

Lemon Dill Fish

1/2 c. mayonnaise or salad
    dressing
2 T. lemon juice
1/2 tsp. grated lemon peel
1 tsp. dried dill weed
1 lb. fish fillets (such as cod,
    flounder, or catfish)

Stir mayonnaise, lemon juice, peel, and dill until well blended. Place fish on greased grill or broiler pan. Brush with half of sauce. Grill or broil for 5 to 8 minutes; turn and brush with remaining sauce. Continue grilling or broiling 5 to 8 minutes or until fish flakes easily with fork.

4 servings. Per serving: 293 calories, 23 g total fat (3 g saturated), 21 g protein, 2 g carbohydrate, 219 mg sodium, 496 mg potassium, 240 mg phosphorus.

Oven Fried Fish

1 lb. fish fillets
Fresh ground pepper
2 T. oil
$1/3$ c. cornflake crumbs

Wash and dry fillets and cut into serving pieces. Season, dip in oil, and coat with crumbs. Arrange in a single layer in a lightly oiled shallow baking dish. Bake at 500 degrees for 10 minutes without turning or basting.

4 servings. Per serving: 161 calories, 10 g total fat (1 g saturated), 16 g protein, 2 g carbohydrate, 91 mg sodium, 26 mg potassium, 204 mg phosphorus.

Halibut with Wine Sauce

2 (8 oz.) halibut steaks
$1/4$ c. dry white wine
1 tsp. cornstarch
1 T. water
1 tsp. butter
$1/4$ tsp. lemon-pepper seasoning

Place fish steaks in a 9-inch glass pie plate; pour wine over fish. Cover with heavy-duty plastic wrap, and vent. Microwave on HIGH 6 to 7 1/2 minutes or until fish is done, rotating dish a quarter turn after 3 minutes.

Remove fish from dish, reserving cooking liquid; set fish aside, and keep warm. Pour cooking liquid into a 1-c. glass measure. Dissolve cornstarch in 1 T. water. Add cornstarch mixture, butter and lemon-pepper to cooking liquid; stir well. Microwave on HIGH 1 to 11/2 minutes or until slightly thickened; spoon over fish.

6 servings. Per serving: 97 calories, 3 g total fat (1 g saturated), 16 g protein, 1 g carbohydrate, 64 mg sodium, 347 mg potassium, 169 mg phosphorus.

Hawaiian Halibut

2 lb. halibut fillets
6 slices canned pineapple
1/4 c. low-salt soy sauce
1/2 T. brown sugar
2 T. oil
1 tsp. flour
1/2 c. dry white wine
1/2 tsp. dry mustard

In a small saucepan, combine soy sauce, brown sugar, oil, flour, wine, and mustard. Bring to a boil, reduce heat, and simmer for 3 minutes. Allow to cool. Marinate fillets for at least 15 minutes. Brush pineapple with the marinade and place with the fish in an oiled broiling pan. Broil 5 to 6 inches from the heat for about 5 minutes on each side, or until fish is done. Remove to a warm platter and spoon sauce over fish and fruit.

12 servings. Per serving: 140 calories, 4 g total fat (1 g saturated), 15 g protein,
6 g carbohydrate, 215 mg sodium, 427 mg potassium, 192 mg phosphorus.

Lemon-Chive Halibut

1 1/2 lb. halibut fillets
Fresh ground pepper
3 T. minced chives
2 T. grated lemon peel
3 T. butter or margarine

Arrange fish in a 2 qt. greased baking dish. Sprinkle with pepper, chives, and lemon peel; dot with butter. Bake, basting once or twice, at 350 degrees for 12 to 15 minutes. Serve with pan juices spooned on top.

8 servings. Per serving: 139 calories, 7 g total fat (3 g saturated), 17 g protein,
0 g carbohydrate, 96 mg sodium, 439 mg potassium, 215 mg phosphorus.

Orange Roughy with Cucumber Relish

1 can (11 oz.) mandarin oranges,
    drained
1 small cucumber, peeled, seeded,
    and chopped
$1/3$ c. white vinegar
1 green onion, minced
1 T. snipped fresh dill
$1 1/2$ lb. orange roughy fillets

Reserve 6 orange sections for garnish, coarsely chop remaining sections and combine with cucumber, vinegar, onion, and dill. Cover, let stand 1 hour, stirring occasionally.

Spray broiler pan with nonstick cooking spray; place fish on pan. Spoon 1 T. of juice from cucumber mixture over fillets. Broil, 3 to 4 inches from heat source, 8 to 10 minutes or until fish is cooked. to serve, spoon cucumber relish on top of fish. Garnish with reserved orange sections.

8 servings. Per serving: 99 calories, 1 g total fat (0 g saturated), 17 g protein,
6 g carbohydrate, 72 mg sodium, 455 mg potassium, 230 mg phosphorus.

BBQ Butterflied Salmon

1 6-8 lb. salmon
3 T. butter or more
3/4 c. butter
1 1/2 T. low-salt soy sauce
1/3 c. sherry
2 cloves minced garlic
1 1/2 tsp. dry mustard
3 T. catsup

Trim salmon of head, slit the underside, and remove bones. Lay salmon out, skin-side down, on heavy-duty foil. Place on grill over a slow fire and brush with at least 3 tablespoons butter. Check after 20 minutes and then every 5 minutes thereafter. When done, the salmon will flake easily with a fork in the thickest places. To serve, lift pieces of salmon with a fork or spatula from the foil. Combine the remaining ingredients and simmer. Serve salmon with sauce.

12 servings. Per serving: 361 calories, 24 g total fat (11 g saturated), 31 g protein, 2 g carbohydrate, 278 mg sodium, 782 mg potassium, 313 mg phosphorus.

Best-Ever Grilled Salmon Fillet

1 lb. salmon fillets (w/skin)
1/8 c. olive oil
1 1/2 T. reduced sodium soy sauce
1 T. lemon juice
1 tsp. minced garlic
1/4 tsp. dried thyme

Place salmon fillets in a glass casserole dish. Combine remaining ingredients and pour over salmon. Marinate one hour, turning fish occasionally.

Prepare the barbecue. Cover barbecue grate with aluminum foil. Remove fillets from dish, reserving the marinade, and place skin-side down on the foil. Basting with remaining marinade, grill fish over medium heat 20 to 25 minutes until fish flakes easily with a fork. Do not turn fish. When fillets are cooked, you can transfer them to a serving platter, leaving the skin behind on the foil.

6 servings. Per serving: 150 calories, 9 g total fat (1 g saturated), 15 g protein,
1 g carbohydrate, 96 mg sodium, 376 mg potassium, 152 mg phosphorus.

Salmon Coriander

1 1/2 lb. salmon fillets
Fresh ground pepper
1 tsp. ground coriander seeds
2 tsp. finely chopped parsley
3 T. butter or margarine

Heat oven to 350 degrees. Grease a 12 x 8-inch baking dish. Season fish with pepper. Arrange in a single layer in dish. Sprinkle with coriander and parsley; dot with butter. Bake, basting once or twice, 15 to 17 minutes. Serve with juices.

8 servings. Per serving: 160 calories, 10 g total fat (4 g saturated), 17 g protein,
0 g carbohydrate, 82 mg sodium, 423 mg potassium, 172 mg phosphorus.

Broiled Shrimp

$1/2$ c. oil
$1^1/2$ tsp. chili powder
$1/4$ tsp. fresh ground pepper
2 cloves minced garlic
3 T. minced parsley
2 T. lemon juice
2 lb. raw shrimp, shelled and
    deveined

Mix together the oil, chili powder, pepper, garlic, parsley, and lemon juice. Marinate the shrimp in the mixture for at least 4 hours; baste and turn occasionally. Arrange shrimp (undrained) in broiling pan. Broil 4 minutes on each side.

> 8 servings. Per serving: 207 calories, 15 g total fat (1 g saturated), 18 g protein, 1 g carbohydrate, 191 mg sodium, 176 mg potassium, 117 mg phosphorus.

Japanese Fried Shrimp

24 lg. fresh shrimp,
    washed and cleaned
$1/2$ c. flour
2 egg whites
2 c. low-salt cornflake crumbs
Cooking oil

Dip each shrimp in flour until completely coated; dip in egg white. roll in cornflake crumbs. Deep fat fry in oil until golden brown.

> 24 servings. Per serving: 92 calories, 5 g total fat (0 g saturated), 3 g protein, 10 g carbohydrate, 112 mg sodium, 31 mg potassium, 21 mg phosphorus.

Sauteed Shrimp

2 T. oil
1½ lb. shrimp, cleaned
¾ c. chopped onions
½ tsp. fresh ground pepper
¼ tsp. marjoram
1 c. dry white wine
2 T. minced parsley

Heat oil in a skillet; saute the shrimp 3 minutes, shaking the pan frequently. Mix in the onions, pepper, marjoram, and wine. Cover and cook over low heat 5 minutes. Sprinkle with parsley.

6 servings. Per serving: 157 calories, 5 g total fat (1 g saturated), 18 g protein, 2 g carbohydrate, 188 mg sodium, 216 mg potassium, 123 mg phosphorus.

Shrimp Curry

2 med. onions, diced
2 med. apples, diced
¼ c. oil
6 T. or more flour
2 T. curry powder
1 qt. low-salt chicken broth
2" piece ginger, minced
2 cloves minced garlic
2 lb. shrimp, cooked

Heat oil in large pan; cook apples and onions until tender (covered). Mix in flour and curry powder; gradually add chicken broth, stirring constantly. Add ginger and garlic. Cover, simmer for 1 hour, stirring often. Push mixture through a colander to make a puree. Reheat in a double broiler and add the shrimp. Thin with a little milk if necessary. Serve over rice.

8 servings. Per serving: 213 calories, 9 g total fat (1 g saturated), 20 g protein, 14 g carbohydrate, 242 mg sodium, 269 mg potassium, 139 mg phosphorus.

Shrimp Scampi

2 lb. unpeeled large shrimp
3 T. butter
1 c. chopped sweet red pepper
8 cloves garlic, crushed
½ c. dry white wine
½ c. minced fresh parsley
¼ c. fresh lemon juice
¼ tsp. pepper
Paprika
8 c. hot cooked angel hair pasta

Peel shrimp, leaving tails intact. Starting at tail end, butterfly underside of each shrimp, cutting to, but not through back of shrimp. Divide shrimp among 8 gratin dishes, arranging shrimp with cut sides up.

Melt butter in a skillet over medium heat. Add red pepper and garlic; sauté 2 minutes. Remove from heat; stir in wine and next 3 ingredients. Spoon over shrimp; sprinkle with paprika. Place dishes on a broiler pan; broil 51/2 inches from heat 6 minutes or until shrimp turn pink. Serve with pasta.

8 servings. Per serving: (w/ 1 c. pasta:) 377 calories, 7 g total fat (3 g saturated), 30 g protein, 44 g carbohydrate, 217 mg sodium, 330 mg potassium, 320 mg phosphorus.

Shrimp Zip

1½ lb. shrimp
1 clove minced garlic
6 green onions, minced
½ green pepper, chopped
1 T. oil
½ c. dry white wine
¼ tsp. Tabasco
¼ tsp. dry mustard
½ c. dry bread crumbs

Cook shrimp for 15 minutes in boiling water; set aside to cool in cooking water. Shell and remove veins; place in casserole or individual baking dishes. Cook and stir vegetables in hot oil for 2 minutes. Add wine, Tabasco, and dry mustard; simmer for 10 minutes. Pour sauce over shrimp; top with bread crumbs. Bake at 425 degrees for 15 minutes.

6 servings. Per serving: 154 calories, 4 g total fat (0 g saturated), 19 g protein,
7 g carbohydrate, 261 mg sodium, 217 mg potassium, 132 mg phosphorus.

Stir-Fry Shrimp

½ c. dry white wine
1 lb. med. shrimp, cleaned
6 green onions, chopped
¼ lb. snow peas
¾ tsp. basil
1 tsp. chopped parsley
1 bay leaf
⅛ tsp. garlic powder
2 T. water
1½ tsp. cornstarch
1 tsp. lime juice
1 T. low-salt soy sauce
⅛ tsp. pepper
Hot cooked rice

Combine wine and shrimp in large skillet; cover and cook over medium heat 5 minutes, stirring occasionally. Add green onions, snow peas, basil, parsley, bay leaf, and garlic powder to skillet. Stir fry 2 to 3 minutes. Combine water and cornstarch in small bowl; add lime juice, soy sauce, and pepper. Add cornstarch mixture to shrimp, stirring well; bring to a boil and cook until slightly thickened, stirring constantly. Remove and discard bay leaf. Serve with rice.

4 servings. Per serving: 127 calories, 1 g total fat (0 g saturated), 19 g protein, 5 g carbohydrate, 2=317 mg sodium, 275 mg potassium, 137 mg phosphorus.

Sweet and Sour Shrimp

2 lb. shrimp
3 T. butter or margarine
2½ c. pineapple chunks
1 green pepper, sliced
½ c. vinegar
½ c. sugar
1 T. low-salt soy sauce
2½ T. cornstarch

Clean and shell shrimp. Heat butter in pan; toss in shrimp and cook about 2 minutes. Pour in pineapple, with juice, green pepper, vinegar, sugar and soy sauce. Cook over low heat about 2 minutes. Spoon out a little of the liquid to mix with cornstarch and make a smooth paste. Pour this back into the shrimp mixture. Cook slowly, stirring constantly, until mixture is transparent and slightly thickened. Serve with rice.

8 servings. Per serving: 234 calories, 5 g total fat (3 g saturated), 18 g protein, 29 g carbohydrate, 294 mg sodium, 284 mg potassium, 122 mg phosphorus.

Sole Meuniere

1 lb. sole fillets
¼ c. flour
¼ tsp. white pepper
3 T. butter or margarine
1 T. minced parsley
2 tsp. lemon juice

Wash and dry fillets. Dip in mixture of flour and pepper. Melt half the butter in a skillet; cook the fish in it until browned on both sides. Transfer to a platter and keep warm. Pour off the fat and wipe the skillet with paper towels. Melt the remaining butter in skillet until it begins to turn brown. Stir in the parsley and lemon juice. Pour over fish.

6 servings. Per serving: 147 calories, 7 g total fat (4 g saturated), 17 g protein, 4 g carbohydrate, 119 mg sodium, 268 mg potassium, 145 mg phosphorus.

Lime and Garlic Snapper

1½ lb. red snapper fillets
⅓ c. olive oil
2 tsp. minced garlic
¼ tsp. crushed red pepper
3 limes, cut in thin wedges
Fresh Chinese parsley leaves

Heat oven to 350 degrees. Grease a 12 x 8-inch baking dish. Wipe fish dry. Arrange in a single layer in prepared dish. Mix oil, garlic, and crushed red pepper; spoon over fish. Bake, basting once or twice with pan juices, 12 to 15 minutes until done. Lift fish onto warm serving plates. Spoon pan juices on top. Garnish plates with lime wedges and Chinese parsley. Squeeze on lime juice and add parsley to taste.

8 servings. Per serving: 177 calories, 11 g total fat (2 g saturated), 18 g protein, 3 g carbohydrate, 56 mg sodium, 386 mg potassium, 174 mg phosphorus.

Red Snapper Floridian

3 T. lemon juice
1 T. white-wine or regular
    Worcestershire sauce
Pepper to taste
1 lb. red snapper fillets
¼ c. butter or margarine
⅓ c. flour
2 egg whites + 1 T. water

Mix lemon juice, Worcestershire, and pepper in shallow dish. Add fish, torn to coat. Cover and refrigerate 1 to 2 hours or overnight. Drain fish. Melt butter in a large ovenproof skillet over medium heat. Coat fish with flour; shake off excess. Dip both sides in egg mixture. Put into skillet skin side up. Cook 3 minutes; turn fillets and remove from heat. Place in oven and bake 10 minutes or until fish is opaque in thickest part.

6 servings. Per serving: 178 calories, 9 g total fat, (5 g saturated), 17 g protein, 6 g carbohydrate, 145 mg sodium, 353 mg potassium, 162 mg phosphorus.

Parsley-Lemon Tuna

1½ lb. tuna fillets
⅓ c. olive oil
½ c. minced fresh parsley
1½ T. fresh lemon juice
2 tsp. minced garlic
¼ tsp. crushed red pepper

Heat oven to 350 degrees. Grease a 12 x 8-inch baking dish. Wipe fish dry. Arrange in a single layer in prepared dish. Mix oil, 1/4 cup of the parsley, lemon juice, garlic, and red pepper; spoon over fish. Bake, basting once or twice with pan juices, 12 to 15 minutes until done. Lift fish onto serving plates. Spoon baking juices on top; sprinkle each with some of the remaining parsley.

6 servings. Per serving: 273 calories, 18 g total fat (3 g saturated), 27 g protein, 1 g carbohydrate, 47 mg sodium, 322 mg potassium, 294 mg phosphorus.

Chapter 8

VEGETABLES AND SIDE DISHES

"*Vegetable Dialysis*": Potassium content of some vegetables can be decreased significantly by the following methods: *Potatoes, beets, carrots:* Peel and slice 1/8 to 1/4 inch thick. Place in 1 to 2 quarts water (depending on portion size), let stand in refrigerator 24 hours. Drain and add fresh water to cover vegetables. Cook until tender. If potatoes are to be fried, cook only 5 minutes to retain shape and firmness.

Frozen green beans, asparagus, cabbage, cauliflower, eggplant, broccoli, okra, summer squash: Let thaw at room temperature. Rinse in running water. Place in 2 to 3 quarts of water at room temperature; let stand for 2 hours. Rinse and cook in large amount of water until tender.

Fresh vegetables: Clean and slice and treat as above.

Asparagus Vinaigrette

1½ lb. fresh asparagus
½ c. balsamic vinegar
2 T. low-sodium chicken broth
2 T. olive oil
2 tsp. lemon juice
2 T. Dijon mustard
2 T. minced fresh parsley
2 tsp. minced fresh tarragon
1 T. minced fresh chives

Snap tough ends off the asparagus. Steam the asparagus in a metal steamer over boiling water for 6 to 8 minutes until asparagus is tender-crisp and bright green. Drain the asparagus and splash with cold water; set aside. Combine all remaining ingredients to make the vinaigrette; pour over the asparagus and serve.

12 servings. Serving size: 1/2 cup. Per serving: 42 calories, 2 g total fat (0 g saturated), 1 g protein, 5 g carbohydrate, 61 mg sodium, 146 mg potassium, 36 mg phosphorus.

Lemon-Sesame Asparagus

12 oz. fresh asparagus or
  1 (8 oz.) pkg. frozen
1 T. butter or margarine
2 tsp. sesame seeds
2 tsp. lemon juice

Wash and trim fresh asparagus. Cook, covered in boiling water 10 to 15 minutes or till tender-crisp. (Or, cook frozen asparagus according to package directions.) In a small saucepan heat and stir butter and sesame seed over low heat about 5 minutes or till seeds are golden brown. Add lemon juice. Drain asparagus; remove to heated serving dish. Pour lemon mixture over hot asparagus.

4 servings. Serving size: 1/2 cup. Per serving: 54 calories, 4 g total fat (2 g saturated), 2 g protein, 4 g carbohydrate, 39 mg sodium, 137 mg potassium, 56 mg phosphorus.

Crunchy Green Beans

1 T. butter
½ c. soft bread crumbs
2 T. grated Parmesan cheese
2 (9 oz.) pkg. frozen green beans
3 water chestnuts, diced
¼ c. butter
1 tsp. lemon juice
⅓ tsp. dried basil, crushed

Melt 1 T. butter in small pan and add bread crumbs. Heat and stir until crumbs brown lightly. Stir in cheese and st aside. Cook green beans as package directs; drain well. Add remaining ingredients, cover and heat through. Turn into warm serving dish and top with the crumb mixture.

9 servings. Serving size: 1/2 cup. Per serving: 78 calories, 7 g total fat (4 g saturated), 1 g protein, 5 g carbohydrate, 85 mg sodium, 69 mg potassium, 56 mg phosphorus.

Green Beans Lyonnaise

1 lb. fresh green beans or 1 pkg.
    frozen
2 T. butter or margarine
½ c. minced onions
1 tsp. lemon juice
⅛ tsp. pepper
1 T. minced parsley

Cook fresh or frozen green beans in water until tender but firm. Drain well. Melt the butter in a skillet; sauté the onions until browned. Mix in lemon juice, pepper, and parsley. Toss with the beans.

8 servings. Serving size: 1/2 cup. Per serving: 47 calories, 3 g total fat (2 g saturated), 2 g protein, 47 g carbohydrate, 33 mg sodium, 134 mg potassium, 26 mg phosphorus.

Roasted Green Beans

3/4 lb. green beans, boiled to
    tender-crisp
1 small onion, peeled and sliced
    into rings
2 cloves garlic, peeled and thinly
    sliced
1 T. Balsamic vinegar
2 tsp. olive oil
Pepper

Preheat oven to 450 degrees. Put beans in a baking dish large enough to hold them in one layer. Scatter onions and garlic over beans. Drizzle with vinegar and olive oil; stir to coat beans. Bake, uncovered, 10 minutes. Remove from oven and stir. Return to oven and bake 5 minutes longer. Sprinkle with pepper to taste.

    6 servings. Serving size: 1/2 cup. Per serving: 39 calories, 1 g total fat (0 g saturated), 1 g protein, 6 g carbohydrate, 5 mg sodium, 142 mg potassium, 27 mg phosphorus.

Beets with Pineapple

2 T. brown sugar
1 T. cornstarch
1 (9 oz.) can pineapple tidbits,
    undrained
1 T. butter or margarine
1 T. lemon juice
1 lb. can low-sodium sliced beets,
    drained

Combine dry ingredients in saucepan; stir in pineapple. Cook, stirring constantly, until mixture thickens and bubbles; add butter, lemon juice, and beets. Heat through.

    6 servings. Serving size: 1/2 cup. Per serving: 83 calories, 2 g total fat (1 g saturated), 1 g protein, 17 g carbohydrate, 59 mg sodium, 178 mg potassium, 17 mg phosphorus.

Bok Choy with Cumin

3 T. peanut oil
½ tsp. red pepper flakes
2 cloves minced garlic
1 tsp. minced fresh ginger
8 c. bok choy, trimmed, rinsed and
    dried, cut in 1" pieces
¼ tsp. cumin seed, toasted
    and crushed (see note*)

Heat oil in wok or heavy skillet over high heat. Add pepper flakes and cook until dark, about 3 minutes. Using slotted spoon, remove pepper and discard. Stir garlic and ginger into hot oil. Quickly add bok choy and stir-fry 1 minute. Sprinkle with cumin seeds, toss to combine and serve.

Note: Toast cumin seeds in dry skillet over medium-high heat until fragrant, about 3 minutes, then pound lightly with bottom of small heavy pan or meat mallet to crush seeds.

9 servings. Serving size: 1/2 cup. Per serving: 49 calories, 5 g total fat (1 g saturated), 1 g protein, 1 g carbohydrate, 46 mg sodium, 161 mg potassium, 25 mg phosphorus.

Cabbage and Noodles

2 lb. cabbage, shredded
2 onions, diced
⅓ c. butter or margarine
½ lb. cooked wide noodles
Freshly ground pepper

Sauté onion in butter; add cabbage and cook until golden. Add noodles and stir well. Season with pepper and serve.

16 servings. Serving size: 1/2 cup. Per serving: 72 calories, 4 g total fat (3 g saturated), 2 g protein, 8 g carbohydrate, 51 mg sodium, 167 mg potassium, 29 mg phosphorus.

Red Cabbage and Apples

2 T. butter or margarine
6 c. shredded red cabbage
1/4 tsp. fresh ground pepper
1/2 c. minced onions
3 T. cider vinegar
3 T. water
2 c. peeled diced apples
1 T. sugar

In a heavy saucepan melt the butter. Add the cabbage, pepper, onions, vinegar, and water; cover and cook over very low heat 1 hour. Mix in the apples and sugar; recover and cook 1 hour longer. Watch carefully and add a little water if necessary to keep from burning.

12 servings. Serving size: 1/2 cup. Per serving: 66 calories, 1 g total fat (1 g saturated), 1 g protein, 8 g carbohydrate, 24 mg sodium, 111 mg potassium, 19 mg phosphorus.

Red Cabbage and Cranberries

2 lb. red cabbage, shredded
2 c. fresh cranberries
2 apples, peeled and sliced
1 c. dry red wine
1/4 c. cider vinegar
1 T. butter, melted
1/2 c. dark brown sugar
1/4 tsp. nutmeg

Place cabbage, cranberries, and apples in large pot. Combine remaining ingredients in small saucepan and heat to boiling. Pour over cabbage mixture and bring to boil. Cover and cook over low heat for 30 minutes or until tender. Add more water if necessary as it cooks.

16 servings. Serving size: 1/2 cup. Per serving: 66 calories, 1 g total fat (1 g saturated), 1 g protein, 13 g carbohydrate, 17 mg sodium, 181 mg potassium, 30 mg phosphorus.

Sweet-Sour Red Cabbage

1 sm. head red cabbage
½ c. white vinegar
½ c. water
1 tsp. sugar

Cut cabbage as for slaw. Combine with other ingredients in large pot. Simmer till tender for about 20 minutes.

9 servings. Serving size: 1/2 cup. Per serving: 13 calories, 0 g total fat (0 g saturated), 0 g protein, 3 g carbohydrate, 3 mg sodium, 66 mg potassium, 10 mg phosphorus.

Braised Carrots

3 c. thinly sliced carrots
¼ c. water
2 T. butter or margarine
1 tsp. sugar
1 T. minced parsley
¼ tsp. fresh ground pepper

In a skillet, combine the carrots, water, butter, and sugar. Cover and cook over low heat 20 minutes or until tender. Shake the pan frequently until water evaporates and carrots are coated with butter. Sprinkle with parsley and pepper.

6 servings. Serving size: 1/2 cup. Per serving: 61 calories, 4 g total fat (2 g saturated), 0 g protein, 6 g carbohydrate, 59 mg sodium, 184 mg potassium, 26 mg phosphorus.

Candied Carrots

¼ c. butter or margarine
¼ c. jellied cranberry sauce
2 T. sugar
2 pkg. frozen baby carrots, cooked
     as package directs

Combine butter, cranberry sauce, and sugar in skillet; heat till cranberry sauce melts. Add carrots; mix, glazing with sauce. Bake at 350 degrees for 10 minutes.

> 8 servings. Serving size: 1/2 cup. Per serving: 86 calories, 6 g total fat (4 g saturated), 0 g protein, 9 g carbohydrate, 74 mg sodium, 5 mg potassium, 2 mg phosphorus.

Fabulous Carrots

3 c. shredded carrots
3 T. butter or margarine
⅛ tsp. pepper

Place carrots in 1-quart casserole; cover tightly. Do not add water. Bake at 325 degrees for 30 minutes. Remove from oven; add butter and seasonings.

> 6 servings. Serving size: 1/2 cup. Per serving 75 calories, 6 g total fat (3 g saturated), 1 g protein, 5 g carbohydrate, 78 mg sodium, 181 mg potassium, 26 mg phosphorus.

Lemon-Glazed Carrots

5 med. carrots
1 T. butter or margarine
1 T. lemon juice
1/8 tsp. nutmeg
1 T. minced parsley

Quarter carrots. In medium covered saucepan cook carrots in a small amount of boiling water 12 to 15 minutes or just till tender; drain and set aside. In same pan melt butter. Stir in lemon juice and nutmeg. Boil gently, uncovered, for 1 minute. Add carrots; toss gently. Turn into serving bowl; sprinkle with parsley.

9 servings. Serving size: 1/2 cup. Per serving: 29 calories, 1 g total fat (1 g saturated), 1 g protein, 39 g carbohydrate, 27 mg sodium, 135 mg potassium, 19 mg phosphorus.

Mint-Glazed Carrots

2 1/2 c. tiny whole carrots
2 T. mint jelly
1 T. butter or margarine
Parsley

Cook carrots in saucepan until tender; drain. Add jelly and butter. Heat slowly until jelly and butter are melted and carrots are glazed, turning carrots frequently. Garnish with snipped parsley.

5 servings. Serving size: 1/2 cup. Per serving: 76 calories, 2 g total fat (2 g saturated), 1 g protein, 14 g carbohydrate, 79 mg sodium, 199 mg potassium, 26 mg phosphorus.

Pineapple Carrots

½ (8 oz.) can crushed pineapple,
   juice pack
½ c. water
2 c. julienne-cut carrots
1 tsp. cornstarch
1 T. chopped parsley

Drain pineapple, reserving 2 T. juice. In saucepan combine drained pineapple and water. Add carrots. Cover and simmer 12 to 15 minutes or till tender. Combine the reserved pineapple juice and the cornstarch. Add to carrots; cook and stir over low heat till bubbly. Stir in the snipped parsley.

   6 servings. Serving size: 1/3 cup. Per serving: 29 calories, 0 g total fat (0 g saturated),
   1 g protein, 7 g carbohydrate, 14 mg sodium, 145 mg potassium, 18 mg phosphorus.

Carrots A L'Orange

6 c. grated carrots
2 c. sliced green onions
Low-salt chicken broth
4 T. butter or margarine
¾ tsp. fennel
3 T. orange-flavored liqueur

Combine carrots and green onions, and cook over lowest heat in barely enough chicken broth to cover. Continue cooking until liquid is reduced to nothing, stirring occasionally. Add 4 T. butter and fennel; mix well. When ready to serve, stir in orange-flavored liqueur, sprinkle with chopped parsley, and heat thoroughly.

   14 servings. Serving size: 1/2 cup. Per serving: 69 calories, 4 g total fat (2 g saturated),
   1 g protein, 9 g carbohydrate, 69 mg sodium, 195 mg potassium, 27 mg phosphorus.

Fried Corn

1 med. onion, chopped
1 clove garlic, chopped
2 T. butter or margarine
1 lb. can no-salt whole kernel corn,
    drained
Dash pepper

Sauté onion and garlic in butter. Over medium-low heat, add corn and a dash of pepper. Cook for 10 minutes, stirring occasionally.

8 servings. Serving size: 1/2 cup. Per serving: 77 calories, 4 g total fat (2 g saturated),
2 g protein, 12 g carbohydrate, 33 mg sodium, 135 mg potassium, 40 mg phosphorus.

Baked Red Onions

8 red onions
Beer
Butter or margarine
Freshly ground pepper

Marinate onions in enough beer to cover for 30 minutes; cut off a piece from the top of each onion, put in a pat of butter and sprinkle with pepper. Wrap tightly in foil and bake at 350 degrees for 1 hour.

8 servings. Serving size: 1 onion. Per serving: 111 calories, 4 g total fat (2 g saturated),
2 g protein, 13 g carbohydrate, 47 mg sodium, 196 mg potassium, 48 mg phosphorus.

Caramelized Onions

1 T. olive oil
3 large white or yellow onions
(2 lb.) quartered and thinly
sliced
2 to 3 tsp. white wine vinegar
Freshly ground pepper

Heat the oil in a large skillet. Add the onions and cook over medium heat, stirring occasionally, until softened and golden, about 30 minutes. Add the vinegar with pepper to taste and continue cooking until the onions have a rich, caramel color, 5 to 10 minutes longer. Keep onions warm in a skillet or transfer to an over-safe dish and set aside. Reheat before serving.

16 servings. Serving size: 1/3 cup. Per serving: 19 calories, 1 g total fat (0 g saturated), 1 g protein, 3 g carbohydrate, 12 mg sodium, 46 mg potassium, 10 mg phosphorus.

Elegant Onions

5 med. onions
1/2 tsp. sugar
1/2 tsp. pepper
1/3 c. butter or margarine
1/2 c. sherry
2 T. grated Parmesan cheese

Slice onion and season with pepper and sugar. Cook in butter 5 to 8 minutes, or just until tender, separating rings. Add sherry, cook 2 to 3 minutes. Sprinkle with Parmesan cheese.

12 servings. Serving size: 1/2 cup. Per serving: 82 calories, 5 g total fat (3 g saturated), 2 g protein, 5 g carbohydrate, 70 mg sodium, 84 mg potassium, 26 mg phosphorus.

Fabulous Fried Onion Rings

1½ c. flour
1½ c. beer, active or flat,
    cold or warm
3 very large onions
3–4 c. shortening

Combine flour and beer in a large bowl and blend thoroughly, using a whisk. Cover the bowl and allow batter to sit at room temperature for no less than 3 hours. 20 minutes before batter is ready, preheat oven to 200 degrees. Place brown paper (from market bags) or layer of paper towels on a cookie sheet. Carefully peel paper skins from onions so that outside layer of onion is left intact. Cut onions into ¼-inch thick slices. Separate slices into rings and set aside. On top of stove, melt enough shortening in a 10-inch skillet to come 2 inches up sides of pan. Heat shortening to 375 degrees. With metal tongs, dip a few onion rings in batter; place them in hot fat. Fry rings, turning once or twice until golden. Transfer to paperlined cookie sheet. Place on middle rack of preheated oven to keep warm until all onion rings have been fried.

6 servings. Serving size: 1/2 onion. Per serving: 223 calories, 7 g total fat (2 g saturated), 4 g protein, 33 g carbohydrate, 6 mg sodium, 166 mg potassium, 56 mg phosphorus.

Glazed Onions

3/4 lb. very small white onions
2 T. butter or margarine
1 tsp. sugar

Peel the onions, cover with water, and bring to a boil. Cook over low heat 10 minutes or until barely tender. Drain well. Melt the butter in a skillet. Add the onions and sugar; cover and cook over low heat until onions are glazed, shaking the pan frequently.

6 servings. Serving size: 1/3 cup. Per serving: 58 calories, 4 g total fat (2 g saturated), 1 g protein, 6 g carbohydrate, 41 mg sodium, 90 mg potassium, 20 mg phosphorus.

Pea Medley

2 c. shelled fresh peas
    or 1 pkg. frozen peas
1/4 c. sliced green onion
1 pkg. frozen pea pods
1 tsp. butter or margarine
1/8 tsp. thyme, crushed
Dash pepper

Place fresh or frozen shelled peas and green onion in steamer basket. Place basket over boiling water. Cover and steam 5 minutes. Add frozen pea pods; cover and steam about 2 minutes more until tender-crisp. Turn into serving bowl. Add butter, thyme, and pepper; toss to coat.

9 servings. Serving size: 1/3 cup. Per serving: 48 calories, 1 g total fat (0 g saturated), 3 g protein, 8 g carbohydrate, 7 mg sodium, 159 mg potassium, 57 mg phosphorus.

Petite Pois Deluxe

2 T. butter or margarine
1 pkg. frozen pease
2 c. finely shredded lettuce
¼ c. chopped onions
¼ tsp. freshly-ground pepper
Pinch of sweet basil, tarragon or
    fresh mint

Melt butter in saucepan; add frozen peas. Cook very slowly until peas defrost. Do not add water. Add lettuce, onion, pepper, and basil. Mix lightly. Cover with tight-fitting lid; steam for 5 minutes. Serve at once.

8 servings. Serving size: 1/2 cup. Per serving: 51 calories, 3 g total fat (2 g saturated), 2 g protein, 5 g carbohydrate, 55 mg sodium, 78 mg potassium, 31 mg phosphorus.

Italian Vegetable Skillet

¼ c. chopped onion
1 clove minced garlic
2 T. oil
1 med. zucchini, sliced
1 c. frozen corn, thawed
1 sm. green pepper, sliced
½ tsp. basil, crushed
½ tsp. oregano, crushed

In 10-inch skillet cook onion and garlic in oil until onion is tender. Stir in zucchini, corn, green pepper, basil, oregano, and dash pepper. Cook over medium heat, stirring frequently, about 5 minutes or till zucchini is crisp-tender.

8 servings. Serving size: 1/2 cup. Per serving: 68 calories, 4 g total fat, (0 g saturated), 2 g protein, 8 g carbohydrate, 2 mg sodium, 170 mg potassium, 28 mg phosphorus.

Steamed Vegetables Parmesan

1 c. bias-sliced carrots
2 c. cauliflower flowerets
1 sm. green pepper, cut into rings
2 T. butter or margarine
1/8 tsp. nutmeg
2 T. grated Parmesan cheese
1 T. chopped parsley

Place carrots in steam basket. Place basket over boiling water; cover and steam for 8 minutes. Add cauliflower to carrots in basket; cover and steam 10 minutes more. Halve any large pepper rings; add pepper to vegetables in basket; cover and steam for 3 to 5 minutes or till all vegetables are tender. Meanwhile, in small saucepan, melt butter; stir in nutmeg. Transfer vegetables to serving bowl; drizzle with melted butter mixture. Sprinkle with grated Parmesan cheese and parsley.

9 servings. Serving size: 1/2 cup. Per serving: 42 calories, 3 g total fat (2 g saturated), 1 g protein, 3 g carbohydrate, 63 mg sodium, 127 mg potassium, 29 mg phosphorus.

Vegetable Mix

1 lg. onion, chopped
2–3 T. butter or margarine
5 sm. zucchini
1 (16 oz.) can no-salt corn

Sauté onions in butter. Wash and cube zucchini. Combine with onions and drained corn. Sprinkle with pepper. Cover and steam until zucchini is tender.

8 servings. Serving size 1/2 cup. Per serving: 81 calories, 4 g total fat (2 g saturated), 2 g protein, 13 g carbohydrate, 33 mg sodium, 187 mg potassium, 53 mg phosphorus.

Sautéed Zucchini Strips

4 sm. zucchini
3 T. oil
1/4 tsp. fresh ground pepper
1/2 tsp. oregano
1 clove minced garlic
1 T. minced parsley

Scrub zucchini but do not peel. Cut into strips 1/4-inch wide by 2-inches long. Heat oil in a skillet; sauté the zucchini over medium heat until browned on all sides. Add the pepper, oregano, garlic, and parsley. Cook over low heat 5 minutes.

6 servings. Serving size: 1/2 cup. Per serving: 64 calories, 7 g total fat (1 g saturated), 1 g protein, 1 g carbohydrate, 1 mg sodium, 59 mg potassium, 11 mg phosphorus.

Zucchini with Dill

3 med. zucchini, sliced 3/8-inch
  thick (1 lb.)
1/4 c. chopped onion
1 T. butter or margarine
1 T. snipped parsley
1 tsp. lemon juice
1/4 tsp. dried dillweed

In covered saucepan, cook zucchini and onion in small amount of boiling water about 5 minutes or just till tender. Drain; add butter, parsley, lemon juice, dill, and pepper; toss.

8 servings. Serving size: 1/2 cup. Per serving: 23 calories, 2 g total fat (1 g saturated), 1 g protein, 2 g carbohydrate, 17 mg sodium, 151 mg potassium, 20 mg phosphorus.

PASTA AND RICE

Lemon Pasta Toss

6 oz. spaghetti or linguini
2 T. lemon juice
4 T. butter or margarine
¼ c. Parmesan cheese
1 T. chopped parsley

Cook spaghetti according to package directions. Drain and place in serving bowl. Toss with lemon juice. Melt butter and add to spaghetti mixture. Sprinkle with Parmesan cheese and toss well. Garnish with parsley.

6 servings. Serving size: 1/2 cup. Per serving: 199 calories, 9 g total fat (6 g saturated), 5 g protein, 23 g carbohydrate, 157 mg sodium, 41 mg potassium, 79 mg phosphorus.

Orzo with Asparagus and Roasted Garlic

1 head of garlic
1 c. orzo pasta
8 oz. fresh asparagus
1 T. butter
$1/4$ c. reduced sodium chicken
    broth
1 T. finely snipped fresh basil
$1/2$ tsp. dried oregano
$1/4$ tsp. freshly ground pepper

Preheat oven to 425 degrees. Remove most of outer papery skin from garlic, leaving bulb intact. Trim a half inch off the top of bulb to expose the cloves. Wrap garlic in foil; bake for 30 to 35 minutes or until very soft.

Cook orzo according to package directions; drain and keep warm. While orzo is cooking, wash and trim asparagus and cut into 1-inch pieces. Melt butter in skillet over medium heat; add asparagus and stir until coated. Add chicken broth, cover and cook for 3 to 5 minutes or until tender-crisp.

Squeeze out roasted garlic pulp and add to asparagus; stir to combine. Add basil, oregano and black pepper. Cook for 1 to 2 minutes. Add mixture to orzo; toss to mix and serve.

6 servings. Serving size: 1/2 cup. Per serving: 103 calories, 3 g total fat, (1 g saturated), 4 g protein, 17 g carbohydrate, 27 mg sodium, 144 mg potassium, 57 mg phosphorus.

Pasta with Dill

½ (8 oz.) pkg. cream cheese,
   softened
¼ c. hot water
2 t. chopped green onion
1 tsp. lemon juice
½ tsp. dried whole dill
8 oz. pasta, such as rigatoni,
   rotelle, etc.

Beat cream cheese until fluffy. Gradually add hot water, beating until smooth. Stir in onion, lemon juice, and dill. Set aside. Cook pasta according to package directions; drain well. Add pasta to cream cheese mixture, tossing gently.

8 servings. Serving size: 1/2 cup. Per serving: 143 calories, 6 g total fat (3 g saturated),
4 g protein, 18 g carbohydrate, 47 mg sodium, 41 mg potassium, 63 mg phosphorus.

Pasta with Pesto

4 sm. bunches fresh basil or
   2 bunches fresh parsley
1 c. olive oil
2 cloves garlic, peeled
1 T. toasted pine nuts
3 T. Parmesan cheese
3 T. Romano cheese
1 lb. linguini noodles

Wash basil or parsley and dry well. Remove stems. Place in blender with the oil, garlic, pine nuts, and cheeses and reduce to a semi-liquid. Cook linguini according to package directions; drain and toss with pesto sauce. Serve at once.

16 servings. Serving size: 1/2 cup. Per serving: 250 calories, 16 g total fat (2 g saturated),
5 g protein, 23 g carbohydrate, 37 mg sodium, 51 mg potassium, 73 mg phosphorus.

Fried Rice

1 1/2 c. water
1 c. raw rice
2 T. oil
1/2 c. chopped green onion
1/4 tsp. minced garlic
2 T. low-salt soy sauce

Bring water to a boil. Stir in rice, bring to a boil again, cover and cook over low heat 15 minutes or until rice is tender and dry. Chill. Heat oil in a skillet; stir in rice until coated. Mix in green onions and garlic; cook 3 minutes. Blend in soy sauce.

6 servings. Serving size: 1/3 cup. Per serving: 178 calories, 5 g total fat (0 g saturated), 3 g protein, 30 g carbohydrate, 171 mg sodium, 53 mg potassium, 40 mg phosphorus.

Italian Herb Rice

2 T. oil
1/2 c. chopped onion
1/2 c. chopped green pepper
1 clove minced garlic
2 1/4 c. water
1/4 c. dry white wine
3/4 tsp. oregano
3/4 tsp. basil
1/8 tsp. pepper
1 c. raw rice
2 T. chopped parsley
2 T. Parmesan cheese

Heat oil on large pan. Sauté onion, green pepper, and garlic under tender. Stir in next 5 ingredients; cover, bring to a boil. Stir in rice; cover, reduce heat, simmer 20 minutes or until rice is tender and dry. Stir in parsley and cheese.

6 servings. Serving size: 1/2 cup. Per serving: 196 calories, 5 g total fat (1 g saturated), 4 g protein, 31 g carbohydrate, 43 mg sodium, 92 mg potassium, 63 mg phosphorus.

Oven-Steamed Rice

1 c. long-grain rice
2 c. boiling water
2 T. melted butter or margarine

Place rice in 1 quart casserole. Add boiling water and melted butter. Cover casserole. Bake at 350 degrees for 40 to 45 minutes. Recipe may be doubled and baked in a 2 quart casserole. This recipe is especially nice for buffet parties as it may be baked in oven and forgotten for 45 minutes.

6 servings. Serving size: 1/3 cup. Per serving: 158 calories, 4 g total fat (2 g saturated), 3 g protein, 27 g carbohydrate, 42 mg sodium, 35 mg potassium, 42 mg phosphorus.

Pilaf

2 c. long-grain rice
1/4 c. linguini or vermicelli,
   broken in 1-2 inch pieces
1/2 c. butter or margarine
5 c. low-sodium chicken broth
   or stock

Brown the broken linguini or vermicelli in butter until golden brown. Add 2 cups or rice and stir lightly until rice is crisp. Pour in hot chicken broth; cover and steam over low heat for about 30 minutes.

12 servings. Serving size: 1/3 cup. Per serving: 210 calories, 9 g total fat (5 g saturated), 4 g protein, 29 g carbohydrate, 125 mg sodium, 38 mg potassium, 46 mg phosphorus.

Risotto

3 T. oil
1/2 c. minced onion
1 c. raw rice
2 1/2 c. low-salt, hot chicken broth
3 T. minced parsley

Heat oil in a skillet; sauté the onions 5 minutes. Stir in rice intil light brown. Add broth; cook over low heat 20 minutes or until tender and dry. Stir in parsley.

6 servings. Serving size: 1/3 cup. Per serving: 207 calories, 8 g total fat (1 g saturated), 4 g protein, 30 g carbohydrate, 47 mg sodium, 60 mg potassium, 43 mg phosphorus.

Toasted Rice and Pasta Pilaf

1 T. vegetable oil
3/4 c. white long-grain rice
2 oz. thin spaghetti, broken into
    1-inch lengths (2/3 c.)
1 small onion, finely chopped
1 can (13 1/4 oz.) low sodium
    chicken broth
1/2 bay leaf
1/4 c. chopped parsley

Heat oil in heavy, medium size saucepan over medium heat. Add rice and spaghetti; cook, stirring constantly until golden brown, 3 to 5 minutes. Add onion and cook, stirring, 3 minutes longer. Very carefully add broth and bay leaf. Bring to boiling. Lower heat and simmer, covered tightly, until rice is tender and broth is absorbed, 15 to 17 minutes. Remove from heat. Discard bay leaf. Fluff pilaf with fork. Stir in parsley.

5 servings. Serving size: 1/2 cup. Per serving: 182 calories, 4 g total fat (1 g saturated), 5 g protein, 33 g carbohydrate, 36 mg sodium, 64 mg potassium, 54 mg phosphorus.

Wild Rice with Acini Pepe Pasta

$\frac{1}{2}$ c. uncooked wild rice
3 quarts plus 1 c. water, divided
$\frac{1}{2}$ lb. (8 oz.) uncooked acini pepe
    pasta*
2 T. butter
$\frac{1}{2}$ c. diced onion
$\frac{3}{4}$ c. sliced mushrooms
$\frac{3}{4}$ tsp dried garlic granules
$\frac{1}{4}$ tsp. black pepper
$2\frac{1}{2}$ tsp. dried basil
*available in gourmet food stores
    or on the internet

Wash wild rice thoroughly; place in a small saucepan with 1 c. water. Bring to boil; simmer covered for about 45 minutes or until tender.

Meanwhile, in a 4 to 6 quart saucepan, bring remaining 3 quarts water to a boil. Add acini pepper pasta and boil 10 to 12 minutes. Drain and set aside.

In a large skillet, melt butter and sauté the onion until translucent. Add the mushrooms and sauté until tender. Add the acini pepe paste, wild rice, garlic granules, pepper and basil. Toss and cook until heated through.

12 servings. Serving size: 1/2 c. Per serving: 111 calories, 1 g total fat (0 g saturated), 4 g protein, 21 g carbohydrate, 8 mg sodium, 76 mg potassium, 58 mg phosphorus.

SIDE DISHES AND RELISHES

Maple Applesauce

¾ c. apple juice
¼ c. water
2 T. maple syrup
½ tsp. Dijon mustard
1 med. apple, chopped
1 T. cornstarch
1 T. water
2 T. vinegar

Combine first 4 ingredients in saucepan; add apple. Bring to a boil. Cover, reduce heat, simmer 4 minutes. Dissolve cornstarch in 1 tablespoon of water; add to apple mixture. Bring to a boil; cook 1 minute or until thickened, stirring constantly. Remove from heat, stir in vinegar. Serve with pork or poultry.

4 servings. Serving size: 1/3 cup. Per serving: 79 calories, 0 g total fat (0 g saturated), 0 g protein, 20 g carbohydrate, 20 mg sodium, 128 mg potassium, 7 mg phosphorus.

Scalloped Apples

6 apples, peeled and sliced thin
1/2 tsp. nutmeg
1 c. sugar
8 oz. sweet butter or margarine
1/4 tsp. cinnamon
4 c. soft bread crumbs

Melt butter and mix with bread crumbs. Mix apples, spices and sugar. Put half the buttered crumbs into small shallow baking dish (9" square), then spread apples over crumbs and top with other half of crumbs. Cover and bake at 350 degrees 40 minutes. Remove cover and bake additional 5 to 10 minutes to brown top. Can be served as a side dish or used as dessert topped with whipped cream.

16 serving. Serving size: 1/2 cup. Per serving: 208 calories, 12 g total fat (7 g saturated), 1 g protein, 25 g carbohydrate, 174 mg sodium, 71 mg potassium, 18 mg phosphorus.

Cabbage-Pepper Relish

3 c. shredded cabbage
1 chopped green pepper
½ c. vinegar
¼ c. water
½ tsp. celery seeds
¼ tsp. pepper
¼ tsp. paprika
2 tsp. sugar

Combine all ingredients. Marinate for at least 1 hour.

8 servings. Serving size: 1/2 cup. Per serving: 19 calories, 0 g total fat (0 g saturated), 1 g protein, 4 g carbohydrate, 5 mg sodium, 105 mg potassium, 9 mg phosphorus.

Pickled Cabbage

¹/₂ head cabbage, grated
1 green pepper, grated
1 carrot, grated
2 green onions, grated
Pepper taste

Dressing

4 T. vinegar
1¹/₂ T. sugar or equivalent
    sugar substitute
³/₄ c. water

Mix all vegetables, adding pepper to taste. Mix dressing; combine with vegetables. Chill before serving.

9 servings. Serving size: 1/2 cup. Per serving: 29 calories, 0 g total fat (0 g saturated), 1 g protein, 7 g carbohydrate, 13 mg sodium, 181 mg potassium, 18 mg phosphorus.

Cranberry-Onion Relish

1 T. oil
¹/₄ c. chopped onion
1 clove minced garlic
1 c. fresh or frozen cranberries
3 T. sugar
1 T. water
1 tsp. cider vinegar

Heat oil in a small saucepan over medium-high heat. Add onion and garlic; sauté until tender. Add cranberries, sugar and 1 T. water. Bring to a boil; cook 3 to 5 minutes or until mixture is thickened. Stir in vinegar. Store in an airtight container and refrigerate. Serve at room temperature.

8 servings. Serving size: 2 T. Per serving: 42 calories, 2 g total fat (0 g saturated), 0 g protein, 7 g carbohydrate, 0 mg sodium, 19 mg potassium, 3 mg phosphorus.

Chapter 9

DESSERTS

Ladyfinger Cake

1 pkg. ladyfingers, split and
    cut in half
8 oz. cream cheese
3/4 c. sugar
2 c. nondairy whipped topping
1 tsp. vanilla

Beat cream cheese and sugar together. Blend vanilla into whipped topping; blend into softened cream cheese. Line bottom and sides of a spring-form pan with ladyfingers. Pour ½ cheese mixture into pan. Top with ladyfingers. Top that with remaining cheese mixture. Refrigerate overnight. Top with raspberries or strawberries.

16 servings. Serving size: 1″ slice. Per serving" 155 calories, 8 g total fat (3 g saturated), 2 g protein, 18 g carbohydrate, 58 mg sodium, 30 mg potassium, 34 mg phosphorus.

Pound Cake

  8 oz. sweet margarine
  1 c. sugar
  4 large eggs, separated
  1 c. + 2 T. sifted cake flour
  1 c. cornstarch, sifted
  1 tsp. grated lemon rind

Line a 9-inch loaf pan with waxed paper on bottom only; do not grease pan. Sift cake flour and cornstarch separately. Measure and sift both together. In large bowl cream softened margarine; add sugar gradually. Beat until white, at least 12–15 minutes. Add egg yolks one at a time; continue beating until fluffy. Add the flour mixture in four additions. Blend after each. Beat egg whites until soft peaks form; fold into batter. Pour into loaf pan. Bake at 350 degrees for 1 hour 10 minutes or until inserted knife comes out clean. Turn out onto wire rack to cool.

16 servings. Serving size: 1/2″ 1 slice. Per serving: 223 calories, 13 g total fat (3 g saturated), 2 g protein, 25 g carbohydrate, 17 mg sodium, 26 mg potassium, 31 mg phosphorus.

Sopa Boracha

  1 pound cake or plain loaf cake,
   cut in 1" slices
  1 tsp. cinnamon
  1 c. rum or brandy
  $1/2$ c. sugar
  $1 1/4$ c. water

Place cake slices in large flat dish or individual flat serving dishes. Sprinkle with cinnamon; pour 3 to 4 T. rum or brandy on each cake slice. Make syrup from sugar and water; boil about 10 minutes. Pour over cake when ready to serve.

12 servings. Serving size: 1″ slice. Per serving: 305 calories, 13 g total fat (8 g saturated), 3 g protein, 34 g carbohydrate, 154 mg sodium, 38 mg potassium, 45 mg phosphorus.

Apricot Jam Squares

2 c. flour
8 oz. sweet butter
2 egg yolks
1 tsp. vanilla
3/4 c. brown sugar
1 jar (10 oz.) apricot jam

Combine first 5 ingredients and blend well. Press dough into jelly roll pan. Coat with jam. Bake at 350 degrees for 30 minutes. Score in squares and return to oven with heat off for 15 minutes.

16 servings. Serving size: 1 square. Per serving: 236 calories, 12 g total fat (7 g saturated), 2 g protein, 30 g carbohydrate, 130 mg sodium, 68 mg potassium, 32 mg phosphorus.

Egg Kichlach

3 eggs
5 T. sugar
3/4 c. oil
1 c. flour

Beat eggs well. Add sugar, beating constantly. Add oil and flour. Drop by scant tablespoons on greased cookie sheet. Bake at 375 degrees for 20 minutes. Remove immediately from cookie sheet.

16 servings. Serving size: 1 cookie. Per serving: 148 calories, 11 g total fat (1 g saturated), 2 g protein, 10 g carbohydrate, 12 mg sodium, 20 mg potassium, 25 mg phosphorus.

Butter 'n Jam Cookies

1 c. butter or margarine
1/2 c. sugar
2 1/2 c. unsifted flour
3 egg yolks
Raspberry jam
Powdered sugar

Cream softened butter, sugar, and yolk thoroughly. Add flour slowly. Work dough until creamy and smooth. Roll small amount into a ball. Put on cookie sheet and press centers with thumb. Bake at 375 degrees until pale pink. Remove from oven, fill centers with raspberry jam and sprinkle with powdered sugar.

30 servings. Serving size: 1 cookie. Per serving: 115 calories, 7 g total fat (4 g saturated), 1 g protein, 12 g carbohydrate, 64 mg sodium, 16 mg potassium, 21 mg phosphorus.

Angel Lemon Bars

1 16 oz. package angel food cake
   mix or a lemon custard angel
   food cake mix, dry
1 22 oz. can lemon pie filling
Powdered sugar glaze or icing,
   optional

Preheat oven to 350 degrees. Place cake mix in bowl and add lemon pie filling; stir until well mixed. Pour into a greased and floured 10-by-13-inch cake pan. Bake 20 to 25 minutes, or until cake springs back when pressed. Cool slightly and frost with powdered sugar glaze Cut into 54 squares.

54 servings. Serving size: 1 square. Per serving: 72 calories, 1 g total fat (0 g saturated), 1 g protein, 15 g carbohydrate, 71 mg sodium, 25 mg potassium, 36 mg phosphorus.

Lemon Bars

    c. flour
$1/2$ c. powdered sugar
1 c. butter or margarine
4 eggs, beaten
2 c. sugar
$1/3$ c. lemon juice
$1/2$ tsp. baking powder

Sift together 2 cups of the flour and 1/2 cup powdered sugar. Cut in butter until mixture clings together. Press into bottom of ungreased 13 x 10 x 2 baking pan. Bake at 350 degrees for 20-25 minutes.

    Beat together eggs, granulated sugar and lemon juice. Sift together 1/4 cup flour and baking powder and stir into egg mixture. Pour over baked crust. Bake at 350 degrees for 25 minutes. Sprinkle with additional powdered sugar. Cool and cut into squares. Makes about 30 squares.

    30 servings. Serving size: 1 square. Per serving: 156 calories, 7 g total fat (4 g saturated), 2 g protein, 23 g carbohydrate, 79 mg sodium, 23 mg potassium, 24 mg phosphorus.

Melting Moments

$3/4$ c. butter or margarine
$2/3$ c. powdered sugar
$1 1/2$ c. flour
$1/2$ c. cornstarch

Cream butter and sugar. Add flour and cornstarch; mix well. Roll dough into walnut-sized balls; place on lightly greased cookie sheet. Flatten slightly with fork. Bake at 350 degrees about 15 minutes or until light brown. 36 cookies.

    18 servings. Serving size: 2 cookies. Per serving: 134 calories, 8 g total fat (5 g saturated), 1 g protein, 15 g carbohydrate, 79 mg sodium, 14 mg potassium, 14 mg phosphorus.

Raspberry Snow Bars

$3/4$ c. shortening
$1/4$ c. sugar
$1/2$ tsp. almond extract
2 eggs, separated
$1 1/2$ c. sifted flour
1 c. raspberry jam
$1/8$ c. sugar

Preheat oven to 350 degrees. Cream shortening and $1/4$ c. sugar until fluffy. Mix in flour. Pat dough into ungreased 13 x 9 x 2 inch pan. Bake for 15 minutes. Spread hot crust with jam. Beat egg white until foamy. Gradually beat in $1/2$ c. sugar until stiff peaks form. Spread over jam. Bake 25 minutes and cool completely on rack. Cut into 24 bars.

24 servings. Serving size: 1 bar. Per serving: 136 calories, 7 g total fat (2 g saturated), 1 g protein, 18 g carbohydrate, 12 mg sodium, 26 mg potassium, 15 mg phosphorus.

Elephant Ear Cookies

$1/4$ c. sugar, divided
1 $17 1/2$ ounce package frozen puff
   pastry sheets thawed

Sprinkle work surface with 1 T. sugar. Place 1 sheet thawed puff pastry on sugar; sprinkle 1 T. sugar over puff pastry sheet. Roll puff pastry to 14-by-10-inch rectangle, pressing in as much sugar as possible. Fold long sides of dough to center. Fold dough crosswise in half to make a rectangle about 7-by-5 inches. Fold dough lengthwise in half to make 7-by-$2 1/2$ inch rectangle. Wrap in plastic wrap, chill in freezer 15 minutes. Meanwhile, repeat with remaining sheet of puff pastry.

Preheat oven to 375 degrees. Cut on rectangle crosswise into $1/2$-inch-thick slices. Place slices, cut side up, 1 inch apart on 2 ungreased large cookie sheets. Bake 12 minutes or until cookies are golden, switching cookie sheets on oven racks halfway through baking time. Remove cookies to racks to cool. Repeat with remaining rectangle.

24 servings. Serving size: 2 cookies. Per serving: 122 calories, 8 g total fat (1 g saturated), 2 g protein, 11 g carbohydrate, 52 mg sodium, 13 mg potassium, 12 mg phosphorus.

Romanian Honey Cookies

2 eggs
1 c. sugar
2 c. flour
2 T. honey
½ tsp. baking soda
½ tsp. cinnamon
Pinch of cloves

Mix ingredients together well; knead about 2 minutes. Add small amount of flour, if necessary. Roll out small portions at a time to 1/8-inch thickness. Cut with cookie cutter into desired shapes. Place on greased cookie sheet. Bake at 350 degrees to desired doneness.

15 servings. Serving size: 1 cookie. Per serving: 130 calories, 1 g total fat (0 g saturated), 2 g protein, 29 g carbohydrate, 50 mg sodium, 27 mg potassium, 29 mg phosphorus.

Low-Sodium Pie Crust

1 stick butter or margarine
1 c. flour
1 T. sugar
1 T. cold water

Cut shortening into flour and sugar mixture. Add water. Roll between waxed paper. Shape into pie pan. Bake at 400 degrees for 12 minutes.

10 servings: Serving size: 1/10 pie. Per serving: (w/marg.): 360 calories, 20 g total fat (10 g saturated), 2 g protein, 11 g carbohydrate, 54 mg sodium, 16 mg potassium, 15 mg phosphorus.

Apple Pie in a Bag

Filling
4–6 large apples, peeled and sliced
1/2 c. sugar
1 unbaked low-salt pie shell
2 T. flour
1/2 tsp. nutmeg
1 tsp. cinnamon
Topping
1/2 c. butter or margarine
1/2 c. sugar
1/2 c. flour

Combine filling ingredients and toss with apples, coating well. Spoon into pie shell. Combine topping ingredients and sprinkle over top of pie. Place pie in large brown paper bag (loosely fastened with wooden clothespins). Bake at 425 degrees for 1 hour.

> 10 servings. Serving size: 1/10 pie. Per serving (w/marg.): 229 calories, 20 g total fat (10 g saturated), 3 g protein, 48 g carbohydrate, 188 mg sodium, 109 potassium, 32 mg phosphorus.

Blueberry Pie

3/4 c. white sugar
1/4 c. brown sugar
2 crust 9″ pie shell
2 pints blueberries
Fresh lemon juice
2 tsp. butter or margarine
Milk

Mix sugars; spread a layer of sugar over bottom crust to keep from getting soggy. Add layer for berries, topped by generous sprinkling of sugar and some lemon juice. Repeat alternate layers. Dot with butter. Put well-pricked crust on top. Seal and flute. Brush lightly with milk. Bake at 425 degrees for 10 minutes, or until crust is golden brown. Lower oven to 350 degrees and bake 45-50 minutes more.

> 10 servings. Serving size: 1/10 pie. Per serving (w/marg.): 374 calories, 21 g total fat (5 g saturated), 5 g protein, 49 g carbohydrate, 302 mg sodium, 106 mg potassium, 38 mg phosphorus.

Ultimate Fresh Pineapple Pie

¼ c. sugar
¼ c. cornstarch
¼ tsp. nutmeg
4 c. ripe, dice pineapple
1 T. margarine

Prepare low-salt pastry for double crust 9-inch pie. Mix together dry ingredients and toss with fruit. Turn into pastry-lined pie plate. Dot with margarine. Make several slits in top crust. Cover pie with top pastry; seal and flute edges. Bake at 425 degrees for 15 minutes. Reduce heat to 350 degrees and bake for 40 minutes longer.

10 servings. Serving size: 1/10 pie. Per serving (w/marg.): 373 calories, 22 g total fat (4 g saturated), 4 g protein, 48 g carbohydrate, 199 mg sodium, 103 mg potassium, 36 mg phosphorus.

Frozen Lemon Chiffon Pie

2 eggs, separated
8 T. sugar, divided
½ tsp. lemon rind
¼ c. lemon juice
8 graham crackers, crushed
1½ c. nondairy whipped topping

Cook egg yolks, 6 T. sugar, lemon rind and juice in top of double broiler, stirring constantly until thick. Beat egg whites stiff with 2 T. sugar. Fold into cooked lemon mixture; chill. Butter inside of pie plate or tray. Sprinkle with half of crumbs. Fold topping into chilled lemon mixture; pour into pie plate. Cover with crumbs; freeze.

8 servings. Serving size: 1/8 of pie. Per serving: 138 calories, 5 g total fat (1 g saturated), 2 g protein, 22 g carbohydrate, 56 mg sodium, 33 mg potassium, 28 mg phosphorus.

Apple Crisp

8 c. peeled, sliced apples
6 T. packed brown sugar
6 T. sugar
1/2 tsp. cinnamon
1/4 tsp. nutmeg
2 tsp. lemon juice
3/4 c. flour
6 T. butter or margarine

Spray inside of 2-quart baking dish with nonstick vegetable cooking spray. Combine apple slices, white sugar, cinnamon, nutmeg, and lemon juice in prepared baking dish; stir gently to mix well. Combine flour and brown sugar. Cut in butter until crumbly. Sprinkle over apples. Bake at 375 degrees for 30 to 40 minutes. Serve warm or cold.

12 servings. Serving size: 1 square. Per serving: 164 calories, 6 g total fat (4 g saturated), 1 g protein, 28 g carbohydrate, 60 mg sodium, 112 mg potassium, 17 mg phosphorus.

Apple Turnovers

2¼ c. peeled, chopped Granny
   Smith apples (about 2 medium)
1 tsp. lemon juice
3 T. granulated sugar
1 T. all-purpose flour
½ tsp. ground cinnamon
¼ tsp. ground nutmeg
8 sheets phyllo pastry, thawed if
   frozen
¼ tsp. ground cinnamon
Butter-flavored vegetable cooking
   spray

Cinnamon sugar: 2 tsp. granulated sugar mixed with ¼ tsp. ground cinnamon (optional). Mix first 6 ingredients in a medium size bowl. Place stacked phyllo sheets on flat surface and cut lengthwise in three 4-inch-wide strips. Cover with plastic wrap to keep from drying out.

Place 1 strip on work surface. Lightly coat with vegetable cooking spray. Top with another strip. Mound 1 heaping T. filling at one end about 1 inch from corner. Fold opposite corner at same end over filling, forming a triangle. Continue folding your way up the strip, as you would a flag, to the end. Repeat with remaining strips of phyllo and filling. (May be made ahead to this point and frozen on a tray or cookie sheet. When firm, pack in plastic bags.)

To bake freshly made or frozen turnovers: Heat oven to 400 degrees. Lightly coat a cookie sheet with vegetable cooking spray. Arrange turnovers seam-side down on prepared cookie sheet. Lightly spray tops with cooking spray. Sprinkle with cinnamon sugar. Bake 15 to 17 minutes or until golden. Remove to wire rack to cool.

12 servings. Serving Size: 1 turnover. Per serving: 28 calories, 0 g total fat (0 g saturated), 0 g protein, 7 g carbohydrate, 4 mg sodium, 28 mg potassium, 2 mg phosphorus.

Peach-Pineapple Brown Betty

2 c. drained canned sliced peaches
1 c. drained crushed pineapple
1/4 c. lemon juice
1 T. tapioca
2 T. sugar
2 slices white bread
5 T. sugar
2 tsp. cinnamon
2 T. melted margarine

Drain fruit, add lemon juice, tapioca, and 3 T. sugar. Put into glass loaf pan. Crumble bread to fine crumbs, add 5 T. sugar, cinnamon, and margarine; mix well. Sprinkle crumb mixture evenly over fruit. Bake at 375 degrees for 45 minutes. Serve warm or cold.

8 servings. Serving size: 1 square. Per serving: 140 calories, 3 g total fat (1 g saturated), 1 g protein, 29 g carbohydrate, 39 mg sodium, 138 mg potassium, 21 mg phosphorus.

Blueberry Streusel Tarts

1 1/2 c. sifted flour
1 tsp. sugar
1/2 c. oil
2 T. milk
1 pint blueberries

Topping

3/4 c. sugar
3 T. flour
2 T. oil

Sift together flour and sugar. Beat the oil and the milk with fork until creamy. Pour over the flour mixture, tossing with a fork until blended. Divide among 8 3-inch tart pans or muffing pans. Pat until bottom and sides are covered. Fill with berries. Combine topping ingredients until crumbly. Sprinkle over tarts. Bake in a 425 degree oven 45 minutes or until pastry edges are brown. Cool on rack.

8 servings. Serving size: 1 tart. Per serving: 336 calories, 17 g total fat (1 g saturated), 3 g protein, 43 g carbohydrate, 5 mg sodium, 65 mg potassium, 34 mg phosphorus.

Cranberry-Raspberry Tart

3 T. vegetable shortening
1 c. flour
3 T. ice water
1 env. unflavored gelatin
¼ c. cold water
2½ c. cranberries
¾ c. raspberry jam
⅔ c. sugar
2 T. water

Cut shortening into flour until mixture resembles coarse meal. Sprinkle the ice water (1 T. at a time) evenly over surface; stir with a fork until dry ingredients are moistened. Shape into a ball. Roll dough to a 12-inch circle on a lightly floured surface. Place in a 9-inch tart pan with removable bottom; press in bottom and up sides of pan. Trim off excess pastry along edges. Prick bottom of pastry several times with a fork. Bake at 425 degrees for 12 to 15 minutes. Remove from oven and cool on rack.

Sprinkle gelatin over ¼ c. cold water; let stand 5 minutes. Combine cranberries and next 3 ingredients in a nonaluminum saucepan; bring to a boil. Remove from heat and stir in gelatin mixture. Pour mixture into tart shell; chill 4 hours or until set. Remove sides of tart pan; cut tart into wedges to serve.

8 servings. Serving size: 1/8 of tart. Per serving: 257 calories, 5 g total fat (1 g saturated), 2 g protein, 52 g carbohydrate, 19 mg sodium, 68 mg potassium, 20 mg phosphorus.

Blueberry Sorbet

1 pine blueberries
$^3/_4$ c. corn syrup
1 env. unflavored gelatin
$^1/_2$ c. grape juice (room temp.)
$^1/_2$ c. sugar
1 T. lemon juice

In blend or food processor, blend blueberries and corn syrup until smooth. Press mixture through fine sieve to remove skins and seeds. In medium bowl, sprinkle gelatin over grape juice. Let stand 5 minutes to soften. Add 1 cup very hot water and stir until gelatin dissolves, about 3 minutes. Stir in sugar until dissolved. Stir in blueberry mixture and lemon juice.

Pour blueberry mixture into 9 x 9-inch baking pan; cover and freeze until partially frozen, about 3 hours. Spoon pieces of blueberry mixture into food processor; blend until smooth but still frozen. (Or spoon mixture into chilled large bowl and beat with chilled beaters.) Return mixture to pan. Cover and freeze until firm. Yield: 1 quart.

9 servings. Serving size: $3^1/_2$ cup. Per serving: 150 calories, 0 g total fat (0 g saturated), 1 g protein, 39 g carbohydrate, 37 mg sodium, 51 mg potassium, 6 mg phosphorus.

Lime Sherbet

1 c. sugar
2 c. water
$^1/_2$ c. lime juice
Green food coloring

Heat sugar and water until sugar is dissolved. Add lime juice and drop of food coloring, if desired. Cool; freeze for 2 to 3 hours, stirring every 30 minutes for the first 2 hours. Yield: 4 servings.

4 servings. Serving size: 1/2 cup. Per serving: 302 calories, 0 g total fat (0 g saturated), 0 g protein, 53 g carbohydrate, 4 mg sodium, 35 mg potassium, 3 mg phosphorus.

Coffee Gelato

1 T. unflavored gelatin
1/4 c. cold water
1 1/2 c. boiling coffee
1/3 c. sugar
Nondairy whipped topping

Soften gelatin in cold water about 5 minutes. Stir in coffee and sugar until dissolved. Cool. Pour into individual molds and chill until set. Top with whipped cream.

6 servings. Serving size: 1/3 cup. Per serving: 52 calories, 0 g total fat (0 g saturated), 1 g protein, 12 g carbohydrate, 4 mg sodium, 33 mg potassium, 1 mg phosphorus.

Rice and Pineapple Pudding

1 (20 oz.) can sliced pineapple
   in juice
1 c. regular long grain rice
1/2 tsp. grated lemon peel
1/2 c. packed light brown sugar
2 T. margarine

Preheat oven to 350 degrees. Into 2 quart saucepan drain juice from pineapple, add 2 1/2 c. water. Over medium heat, heat juice mixture to boiling. Meanwhile, in 10 x 6-inch baking dish, combine rice and grated lemon peel. Arrange pineapple slices on top. Pour boiling juice mixture over pineapple. Sprinkle with brown sugar, then dot with margarine. Cover with foil and bake 30 minutes. Remove foil; bake 30 minutes longer or until rice is tender.

8 servings. Serving size: 1/2 cup. Per serving: 186 calories, 3 g total fat (1 g saturated), 2 g protein, 39 g carbohydrate, 5 mg sodium, 146 mg potassium, 33 mg phosphorus.

Schaum Torte

> 8 egg whites
> 1 tsp. vinegar
> 1 tsp. vanilla
> 2 c. sugar
> Nondairy whipped topping

Lightly grease and flour, or cover baking sheet with heavy brown paper. Place egg whites in large bowl and beat until foamy. Add vinegar, beating constantly. Gradually add sugar, 2 T, at a time. Add vanilla and continue beating until very stiff and glossy. Shape meringue into individual schaum tortes using back of spoon to build up sides, or shape into two large schaume tortes. Bake at 275 degrees 50 to 60 minutes. To serve, fill with nondairy whipped topping. Top with fresh berries or your favorite sauce.

8 servings: Serving size: 1/8 or torte. Per serving: 214 calories, 0 g total fat (0 g saturated), 4 g protein, 50 g carbohydrate, 55 mg sodium, 50 mg potassium, 5 mg phosphorus.

Strawberry Napoleons

> 3 sheets phyllo pastry
> 2 t. butter or margarine, melted
> 2½ c. nondairy whipped topping
> 2½ c. sliced strawberries

Unfold 3 sheets phyllo according to package directions. Cover loosely with plastic wrap or foil to keep from drying. Place 1 sheet on a 17 x 14-inch cookie sheet. Brush phyllo quickly with butter. Top with remaining 2 sheets, buttering top of each. With a sharp knife, cut four 3¾-inch-wide strips crosswise from stack of sheets. Cut the 4 strips lengthwise into three 4-inch-wide strips. You should have twelve 4 x 3¾-inch rectangles. Bake at 375 degrees for 8 to 10 minutes until lightly browned. Cool on rack. To serve, top with whipped topping and strawberries. Sprinkle with powdered sugar, if desired.

12 servings. Serving size: 1 bar. Per serving: 88 calories, 6 g total fat (1 g saturated), 1 g protein, 8 g carbohydrate, 43 mg sodium, 62 mg potassium, 11 mg phosphorus.

Apple Mousse

1 c. sour cream
2 c. unsweetened applesauce
¼ tsp. cinnamon
Sugar substitute equivalent to
    2 T. sugar

Combine ingredients and chill in individual sherbet glasses.

6 servings. Serving size: 1/2 cup. Per serving: 117 calories, 8 g total fat (5 g saturated),
1 g protein, 11 g carbohydrate, 22 mg sodium, 117 mg potassium, 38 mg phosphorus.

French Apple Tart

1 c. cake flour
2 T. sugar
¼ c. butter or margarine,
 cut up and chilled
2 to 3 T. ice water
1 lb. baking apples, peeled,
 cored and sliced
1 T. honey
¼ tsp. cinnamon

Combine flour and sugar in a large bowl; cut in butter until mixture resembles coarse meal. Sprinkle ice water (1 T. at a time) over surface; toss with a fork until dry ingredients are moistened and mixture is crumbly. (Don't form a ball.) Gently press mixture into a 4-inch circle on heavy-duty plastic wrap; cover with additional plastic wrap, and chill 15 minutes. Roll dough, still covered, to an 11-inch circle; place in freezer 5 minutes or until plastic wrap can easily be removed. Fit dough into a 10-inch round tart pan, and remove plastic wrap. Prick bottom of pastry with a fork. Chill 15 minutes. Bake at 400 degrees for 15 minutes or until pastry is lightly browned.

Arrange sliced apples over pastry. Bake at 400 degrees for 30 minutes or until crust is golden and apples are tender. Combine honey and cinnamon in a small bowl; place bowl in a saucepan of hot water, and cook over low heat until thin. Brush over apples.

8 servings. Serving size: 1/8 or tart. Per serving: 148 calories, 6 g total fat (4 g saturated), 1 g protein, 23 g carbohydrate, 59 mg sodium, 82 mg potassium, 16 mg phosphorus.

Pineapple Fluff

1 pkg. diet lemon gelatin
1¼ c. boiling water
Sugar substitute to equal 2 tsp.
  sugar
2 c. low-cal whipped topping
1 (14 oz.) can pineapple chunks

Drain pineapple, reserving juice. Dissolve gelatin in boiling water. Add enough water to reserved juice to make ¾ cup liquid. Stir into gelatin with noncaloric sweetener; chill until slightly thickened. Blend in whipped topping and pineapple; chill until firm.

8 servings. Serving size: 1/2 cup. Per serving: 45 calories, 1 g total fat (1 g saturated), 1 g protein, 10 g carbohydrate, 50 mg sodium, 66 mg potassium, 25 mg phosphorus.

Rice Fluff

2 c. cooked rice
1 lg. can dietetic fruit cocktail,
  drained
1 env. low calorie whipped
  topping mix, prepared
Sugar substitute to taste

Combine all ingredients; chill for 15 minutes before serving.

6 servings. Serving size: 1/2 cup. Per serving: 111 calories, 0 g total fat (0 g saturated), 2 g protein, 25 g carbohydrate, 4 mg sodium, 82 mg potassium, 33 mg phosphorus.

The Renal Patient's Guide To Good Eating

Strawberry Chiffon Pie

1 pkg. low calorie strawberry
  gelatin
1 env. gelatin, softened in
  1/4 c. cold water
1 envelope low calorie whipped
  topping mix, prepared
8 graham crackers, crushed
4 oz. strawberries, sliced

Make strawberry gelatin according to package directions. Add softened gelatin to hot mixture; stir until dissolved. Cool mixture with ice cubes. Add enough whipped topping to cracker crumbs to hold them together. Press into pie pan. Reserve enough topping to garnish pie top. Combine remaining topping with gelatin mixture and strawberries. Pour into pie shell; garnish with topping and several sliced strawberries.

6 servings. Serving size: 1/6 of pie. Per serving: 42 calories, 1 g total fat (0 g saturated),
2 g protein, 7 g carbohydrate, 73 mg sodium, 34 mg potassium, 27 mg phosphorus.

INDEX